Terence Rattigan

THE DEEP
BLUE SEA

Introduced by
DAN REBELLATO

NICK HERN BOOKS
London

A Nick Hern Book

This edition of *The Deep Blue Sea* first published
as a paperback original in Great Britain in 1999
by Nick Hern Books, 14 Larden Road, London W3 7ST
by arrangement with Methuen. *The Deep Blue Sea* was included
in Volume Two of *The Collected Plays of Terence Rattigan*
published in 1953 by Hamish Hamilton

Copyright © Trustees of the Terence Rattigan Trust 1953
Introduction copyright © Dan Rebellato 1999
Front cover photo copyright © Hulton Deutsch Collection

Typeset by Country Setting. Kingsdown, Kent CT14 8ES
Printed and bound by Athenaeum Press, Gateshead

A CIP catalogue record for this book is available from
the British Library

ISBN 1 85459 423 0

Terence Rattigan

Born in 1911, a scholar at Harrow and at Trinity College, Oxford,
Terence Rattigan had his first long-running hit in the West End
at the age of twenty-five: *French Without Tears* (1936). His next
play, *After the Dance* (1939), opened to euphoric reviews yet
closed under the gathering clouds of war, but with *Flare Path*
(1942) Rattigan embarked on an almost unbroken series of
successes, with most plays running in the West End for at least a
year and several making the transition to Broadway: *While the Sun
Shines* (1943), *Love in Idleness* (1944), *The Winslow Boy* (1946),
The Browning Version (performed in double-bill with
Harlequinade, 1948), *Who is Sylvia?* (1950), *The Deep Blue Sea*
(1952), *The Sleeping Prince* (1953) and *Separate Tables* (1954).
From the mid-fifties, with the advent of the 'Angry Young Men',
he enjoyed less success on stage, though *Ross* (1960) and *In
Praise of Love* (1973) were well received. As well as seeing many
of his plays turned into successful films, Rattigan wrote a number
of original plays for television from the fifties onwards. He was
knighted in 1971 and died in 1977.

Terence Rattigan (1911-1977)

Terence Rattigan stood on the steps of the Royal Court Theatre, on 8 May 1956, after the opening night of John Osborne's *Look Back in Anger*. Asked by a reporter what he thought of the play, he replied, with an uncharacteristic lack of discretion, that it should have been retitled 'Look how unlike Terence Rattigan I'm being.' [1] And he was right. The great shifts in British theatre, marked by Osborne's famous première, ushered in kinds of playwriting which were specifically unlike Rattigan's work. The pre-eminence of playwriting as a formal craft, the subtle tracing of the emotional lives of the middle classes – those techniques which Rattigan so perfected – fell dramatically out of favour, creating a veil of prejudice through which his work even now struggles to be seen.

Terence Mervyn Rattigan was born on 10 June 1911, a wet Saturday a few days before George V's coronation. His father, Frank, was in the diplomatic corps and Terry's parents were often posted abroad, leaving him to be raised by his paternal grandmother. Frank Rattigan was a geographically and emotionally distant man, who pursued a string of little-disguised affairs throughout his marriage. Rattigan would later draw on these memories when he created Mark St Neots, the bourgeois Casanova of *Who is Sylvia?* Rattigan was much closer to his mother, Vera Rattigan, and they remained close friends until her death in 1971.

Rattigan's parents were not great theatregoers, but Frank Rattigan's brother had married a Gaiety Girl, causing a minor family uproar, and an apocryphal story suggests that the 'indulgent aunt' reported as taking the young Rattigan to the theatre may have been this scandalous relation.[2] And when, in the summer of 1922, his family went to stay in the country cottage of the drama critic Hubert Griffiths, Rattigan avidly worked through his extensive library of playscripts. Terry went to Harrow in 1925, and there maintained both his somewhat illicit theatregoing habit and his insatiable reading, reputedly devouring every play in the school library. Apart from contemporary authors like Galsworthy, Shaw and Barrie, he also read the plays of Chekhov, a writer whose crucial influence he often acknowledged.[3]

His early attempts at writing, while giving little sign of his later sophistication, do indicate his ability to absorb and reproduce his own theatrical experiences. There was a ten-minute melodrama about the Borgias entitled *The Parchment*, on the cover of which the author recommends with admirable conviction that a suitable cast for this work might comprise 'Godfrey Tearle, Gladys Cooper, Marie Tempest, Matheson Lang, Isobel Elsom, Henry Ainley . . . [and] Noël Coward'.[4] At Harrow, when one of his teachers demanded a French playlet for a composition exercise, Rattigan, undaunted by his linguistic shortcomings, produced a full-throated tragedy of deception, passion and revenge which included the immortal curtain line: 'COMTESSE. (*Souffrant terriblement.*) Non! non! non! Ah non! Mon Dieu, non!'[5] His teacher's now famous response was 'French execrable: theatre sense first class'.[6] A year later, aged fifteen, he wrote *The Pure in Heart,* a rather more substantial play showing a family being pulled apart by a son's crime and the father's desire to maintain his reputation. Rattigan's ambitions were plainly indicated on the title pages, each of which announced the author to be 'the famous playwrite and author T. M. Rattigan.'[7]

Frank Rattigan was less than keen on having a 'playwrite' for a son and was greatly relieved when in 1930, paving the way for a life as a diplomat, Rattigan gained a scholarship to read History at Trinity, Oxford. But Rattigan's interests were entirely elsewhere. A burgeoning political conscience that had led him to oppose the compulsory Officer Training Corps parades at Harrow saw him voice pacifist and socialist arguments at college, even supporting the controversial Oxford Union motion 'This House will in no circumstances fight for its King and Country' in February 1933. The rise of Hitler (which he briefly saw close at hand when he spent some weeks in the Black Forest in July 1933) and the outbreak of the Spanish Civil War saw his radical leanings deepen and intensify. Rattigan never lost his political compassion. After the war he drifted towards the Liberal Party, but he always insisted that he had never voted Conservative, despite the later conception of him as a Tory playwright of the establishment.[8]

Away from the troubled atmosphere of his family, Rattigan began to gain in confidence as the contours of his ambitions and his identity moved more sharply into focus. He soon took advantage of the university's theatrical facilities and traditions. He joined The Oxford Union Dramatic Society (OUDS), where contemporaries included Giles Playfair, George Devine, Peter Glenville, Angus Wilson and Frith Banbury. Each year, OUDS ran a one-act play competition and in Autumn 1931 Rattigan submitted one. Unusually, it seems that this was a highly experimental effort, somewhat like Konstantin's piece in *The Seagull*. George Devine, the OUDS president, apparently told the young author, 'Some of it is absolutely smashing, but it goes too far'.[9] Rattigan was instead to make his first mark as a somewhat scornful reviewer for the student newspaper, *Cherwell*, and as a performer in the Smokers (OUDS's private revue club), where he adopted the persona and dress of 'Lady Diana Coutigan', a drag performance which allowed him to discuss leading members of the Society with a barbed camp wit.[10]

That the name of his Smokers persona echoed the contemporary phrase, 'queer as a coot', indicates Rattigan's new-found confidence in his homosexuality. In February 1932, Rattigan played a tiny part in the OUDS production of *Romeo and Juliet*, which was directed by John Gielgud and starred Peggy Ashcroft and Edith Evans (women undergraduates were not admitted to OUDS, and professional actresses were often recruited). Rattigan's failure to deliver his one line correctly raised an increasingly embarrassing laugh every night (an episode which he re-uses to great effect in *Harlequinade*). However, out of this production came a friendship with Gielgud and his partner, John Perry. Through them, Rattigan was introduced to theatrical and homosexual circles, where his youthful 'school captain' looks were much admired.

A growing confidence in his sexuality and in his writing led to his first major play. In 1931, he shared rooms with a contemporary of his, Philip Heimann, who was having an affair with Irina Basilevich, a mature student. Rattigan's own feelings for Heimann completed an eternal triangle that formed the basis of the play he co-wrote with Heimann, *First Episode*. This play was accepted for production in Surrey's "Q" theatre; it was respectfully received and subsequently transferred to the Comedy Theatre in London's West End, though carefully shorn of its homosexual subplot. Despite receiving only £50 from this production (and having put £200 into it), Rattigan immediately dropped out of college to become a full-time writer.

Frank Rattigan was displeased by this move, but made a deal with his son. He would give him an allowance of £200 a year for two years and let him live at home to write; if at the end of that period, he had had no discernible success, he would enter a more secure and respectable profession. With this looming deadline, Rattigan wrote quickly. *Black Forest*, an O'Neill-inspired play based on his experiences in Germany in 1933, is one of the three that have survived. Rather unwillingly, he collaborated with Hector Bolitho on an adaptation of the latter's novel, *Grey Farm*, which received a disastrous New York production in 1940. Another project was an adaptation of *A Tale of Two Cities*, written with Gielgud; this fell through at the last minute when Donald Albery, the play's potential producer, received a complaint from actor-manager John Martin-Harvey who was beginning a farewell tour of his own adaptation, *The Only Way*, which he had been performing for forty-five years. As minor compensation, Albery invited Rattigan to send him any other new scripts. Rattigan sent him a play pro-

visionally titled *Gone Away*, based on his experiences in a French
language Summer School in 1931. Albery took out a nine-month
option on it, but no production appeared.

By mid-1936, Rattigan was despairing. His father had secured him
a job with Warner Brothers as an in-house screenwriter, which was
reasonably paid; but Rattigan wanted success in the theatre, and
his desk-bound life at Teddington Studios seemed unlikely to
advance this ambition. By chance, one of Albery's productions
was unexpectedly losing money, and the wisest course of action
seemed to be to pull the show and replace it with something
cheap. Since *Gone Away* required a relatively small cast and only
one set, Albery quickly arranged for a production. Harold French,
the play's director, had only one qualm: the title. Rattigan
suggested *French Without Tears*, which was immediately adopted.

After an appalling dress rehearsal, no one anticipated the
rapturous response of the first-night audience, led by Cicely
Courtneidge's infectious laugh. The following morning Kay
Hammond, the show's female lead, discovered Rattigan
surrounded by the next day's reviews. 'But I don't believe it', he
said. 'Even *The Times* likes it.' [11]

French Without Tears played over 1000 performances in its three-
year run and Rattigan was soon earning £100 a week. He moved
out of his father's home, wriggled out of his Warner Brothers
contract, and dedicated himself to spending the money as soon as
it came in. Partly this was an attempt to defer the moment when
he had to follow up this enormous success. In the event, both of
his next plays were undermined by the outbreak of war.

After the Dance, an altogether more bleak indictment of the Bright
Young Things' failure to engage with the iniquities and miseries of
contemporary life, opened, in June 1939, to euphoric reviews; but
only a month later the European crisis was darkening the national
mood and audiences began to dwindle. The play was pulled in
August after only sixty performances. *Follow My Leader* was a
satirical farce closely based on the rise of Hitler, co-written with
an Oxford contemporary, Tony Goldschmidt (writing as Anthony
Maurice in case anyone thought he was German). It suffered an
alternative fate. Banned from production in 1938, owing to the
Foreign Office's belief that 'the production of this play at this time
would not be in the best interests of the country', [12] it finally
received its première in 1940, by which time Rattigan and
Goldschmidt's mild satire failed to capture the real fears that the
war was unleashing in the country.

Rattigan's insecurity about writing now deepened. An interest in
Freud, dating back to his Harrow days, encouraged him to visit a
psychiatrist that he had known while at Oxford, Dr Keith
Newman. Newman exerted a svengali-like influence on Rattigan

and persuaded the pacifist playwright to join the RAF as a means of curing his writer's block. Oddly, this unorthodox treatment seemed to have some effect; by 1941, Rattigan was writing again. On one dramatic sea crossing, an engine failed, and with everyone forced to jettison all excess baggage and possessions, Rattigan threw the hard covers and blank pages from the notebook containing his new play, stuffing the precious manuscript into his jacket.

Rattigan drew on his RAF experiences to write a new play, *Flare Path*. Bronson Albery and Bill Linnit who had both supported *French Without Tears* both turned the play down, believing that the last thing that the public wanted was a play about the war.[13] H. M. Tennent Ltd., led by the elegant Hugh 'Binkie' Beaumont, was the third management offered the script; and in 1942, *Flare Path* opened in London, eventually playing almost 700 performances. Meticulously interweaving the stories of three couples against the backdrop of wartime uncertainty, Rattigan found himself 'commended, if not exactly as a professional playwright, at least as a promising apprentice who had definitely begun to learn the rudiments of his job'.[14] Beaumont, already on the way to becoming the most powerful and successful West End producer of the era, was an influential ally for Rattigan. There is a curious side-story to this production; Dr Keith Newman decided to watch 250 performances of this play and write up the insights that his 'serial attendance' had afforded him. George Bernard Shaw remarked that such playgoing behaviour 'would have driven me mad; and I am not sure that [Newman] came out of it without a slight derangement'. Shaw's caution was wise.[15] In late 1945, Newman went insane and eventually died in a psychiatric hospital.

Meanwhile, Rattigan had achieved two more successes; the witty farce, *While the Sun Shines*, and the more serious, though politically clumsy, *Love in Idleness* (retitled *O Mistress Mine* in America). He had also co-written a number of successful films, including *The Day Will Dawn, Uncensored, The Way to the Stars* and an adaptation of *French Without Tears*. By the end of 1944, Rattigan had three plays running in the West End, a record only beaten by Somerset Maugham's four in 1908.

Love in Idleness was dedicated to Henry 'Chips' Channon, the Tory MP who had become Rattigan's lover. Channon's otherwise gossipy diaries record their meeting very discreetly: 'I dined with Juliet Duff in her little flat . . . also there, Sibyl Colefax and Master Terence Rattigan, and we sparkled over the Burgundy. I like Rattigan enormously, and feel a new friendship has begun. He has a flat in Albany'.[16] Tom Driberg's rather less discreet account fleshes out the story: Channon's 'seduction of the playwright was almost like the wooing of Danaë by Zeus – every day the playwright found, delivered to his door, a splendid present – a case of champagne, a huge pot of caviar, a Cartier cigarette-box in two kinds of gold . . . In the end, of course, he gave in, saying apologetically to his friends, "How can one *not?*" '.[17] It was a very different set in which Rattigan now moved, one that was wealthy and conservative, the very people he had criticised in *After the Dance*. Rattigan did not share the complacency of many of his friends, and his next play revealed a deepening complexity and ambition.

For a long time, Rattigan had nurtured a desire to become respected as a serious writer; the commercial success of *French Without Tears* had, however, sustained the public image of Rattigan as a wealthy young light comedy writer-about-town. [18] With *The Winslow Boy*, which premièred in 1946, Rattigan began to turn this image around. In doing so he entered a new phase as a playwright. As one contemporary critic observed, this play 'put him at once into the class of the serious and distinguished writer'.[19] The play, based on the Archer-Shee case in which a family attempted to sue the Admiralty for a false accusation of theft against their son, featured some of Rattigan's most elegantly crafted and subtle characterization yet. The famous second curtain, when the barrister Robert Morton subjects Ronnie Winslow to a vicious interrogation before announcing that 'The boy is plainly innocent. I accept the brief', brought a joyous standing ovation on the first night. No less impressive is the subtle handling of the concept of 'justice' and 'rights' through the play of ironies which pits Morton's liberal complacency against Catherine Winslow's feminist convictions.

Two years later, Rattigan's *Playbill*, comprising the one-act plays *The Browning Version* and *Harlequinade*, showed an ever deepening talent. The latter is a witty satire of the kind of touring theatre encouraged by the new Committee for the Encouragement of Music and Arts (CEMA, the immediate forerunner of the Arts Council). But the former's depiction of a failed, repressed Classics teacher evinced an ability to choreograph emotional subtleties on stage that outstripped anything Rattigan had yet demonstrated.

Adventure Story, which in 1949 followed hard on the heels of *Playbill*, was less successful. An attempt to dramatize the emotional dilemmas of Alexander the Great, Rattigan seemed unable to escape the vernacular of his own circle, and the epic scheme of the play sat oddly with Alexander's more prosaic concerns.

Rattigan's response to both the critical bludgeoning of this play and the distinctly luke-warm reception of *Playbill* on Broadway was to write a somewhat extravagant article for the *New Statesman*. 'Concerning the Play of Ideas' was a desire to defend the place of 'character' against those who would insist on the pre-eminence in drama of ideas.[20] The essay is not clear and is couched in such teasing terms that it is at first difficult to see why it should have secured such a fervent response. James Bridie, Benn Levy, Peter Ustinov, Sean O'Casey, Ted Willis, Christopher Fry and finally George Bernard Shaw all weighed in to support or condemn the article. Finally Rattigan replied in slightly more moderate terms to these criticisms insisting (and the first essay reasonably supports this) that he was not calling for the end of ideas in the theatre, but rather for their inflection through character and situation.[21] However, the damage was done (as, two years later, with his 'Aunt Edna', it would again be done). Rattigan was increasingly being seen as the arch-proponent of commercial vacuity.[22]

The play Rattigan had running at the time added weight to his opponents' charge. Originally planned as a dark comedy, *Who is Sylvia?* became a rather more frivolous thing both in the writing and the playing. Rattled by the failure of *Adventure Story*, and superstitiously aware that the new play was opening at the Criterion, where fourteen years before *French Without Tears* had been so successful, Rattigan and everyone involved in the production had steered it towards light farce and obliterated the residual seriousness of the original conceit.

Rattigan had ended his affair with Henry Channon and again taken up with Kenneth Morgan, a young actor who had appeared in *Follow My Leader* and the film of *French Without Tears*. However, the relationship had not lasted and Morgan had for a while been seeing someone else. Rattigan's distress was compounded one day in February 1949, when he received a message that Morgan had killed himself. Although horrified, Rattigan soon began to conceive an idea for a play. The result is one of the finest examples of Rattigan's craft. The story of Hester Collyer, trapped in a relationship with a man incapable of returning her love, and her transition from attempted suicide to groping, uncertain self-determination is handled with extraordinary economy, precision and power. The depths of despair and desire that Rattigan plumbs have made *The Deep Blue Sea* one of his most popular and moving pieces.

1953 saw Rattigan's romantic comedy *The Sleeping Prince*, planned as a modest, if belated, contribution to the Coronation festivities. However, the project was hypertrophied by the insistent presence of Laurence Olivier and Vivien Leigh in the cast and the critics were disturbed to see such whimsy from the author of *The Deep Blue Sea*.

Two weeks after its opening, the first two volumes of Rattigan's *Collected Plays* were published. The preface to the second volume introduced one of Rattigan's best-known, and most notorious creations: Aunt Edna. 'Let us invent,' he writes, 'a character, a nice respectable, middle-class, middle-aged, maiden lady, with time on her hands and the money to help her pass it'.[23] Rattigan paints a picture of this eternal theatregoer, whose bewildered disdain for modernism ('Picasso – "those dreadful reds, my dear, and why three noses?" ')[24] make up part of the particular challenge of dramatic writing. The intertwined commercial and cultural pressures that the audience brings with it exert considerable force on the playwright's work.

Rattigan's creation brought considerable scorn upon his head. But Rattigan is neither patronizing nor genuflecting towards Aunt Edna. The whole essay is aimed at demonstrating the crucial rôle of the audience in the theatrical experience. Rattigan's own sense of theatre was *learned* as a member of the audience, and he refuses to distance himself from this woman: 'despite my already self-acknowledged creative ambitions I did not in the least feel myself a being apart. If my neighbours gasped with fear for the heroine when she was confronted with a fate worse than death, I gasped with them'.[25] But equally, he sees his job as a writer to engage in a gentle tug-of-war with the audience's expectations: 'although Aunt Edna must never be made mock of, or bored, or befuddled, she must equally not be wooed, or pandered to or cosseted'.[26] The complicated relation between satisfying and surprising this figure may seem contradictory, but as Rattigan notes, 'Aunt Edna herself is indeed a highly contradictory character'.[27]

But Rattigan's argument, as in the 'Play of Ideas' debate before it, was taken to imply an insipid pandering to the unchallenging expectations of his audience. Aunt Edna dogged his career from that moment on and she became such a by-word for what theatre should *not* be that in 1960, the Questors Theatre, Ealing, could title a triple-bill of Absurdist plays, 'Not For Aunt Edna'.[28]

Rattigan's next play did help to restore his reputation as a serious dramatist. *Separate Tables* was another double-bill, set in a small Bournemouth hotel. The first play develops Rattigan's familiar themes of sexual longing and humiliation while the second pits a man found guilty of interfering with women in a local cinema against the self-appointed moral jurors in the hotel. The evening was highly acclaimed and the subsequent Broadway production a rare American success.

However, Rattigan's reign as the leading British playwright was about to be brought to an abrupt end. In a car from Stratford to London, early in 1956, Rattigan spent two and a half hours informing his Oxford contemporary George Devine why the new play he had discovered would not work in the theatre. When Devine persisted, Rattigan answered 'Then I know nothing about plays'. To which Devine replied, 'You know everything about plays, but you don't know a fucking thing about *Look Back in Anger.*' [29] Rattigan only barely attended the first night. He and Hugh Beaumont wanted to leave at the interval until the critic T. C. Worsley persuaded them to stay.[30]

The support for the English Stage Company's initiative was soon overwhelming. Osborne's play was acclaimed by the influential critics Kenneth Tynan and Harold Hobson, and the production was revived frequently at the Court, soon standing as the banner under which that disparate band of men (and women), the Angry Young Men, would assemble. Like many of his contemporaries, Rattigan decried the new movements, Beckett and Ionesco's turn from Naturalism, the wild invective of Osborne, the passionate socialism of Wesker, the increasing influence of Brecht. His opposition to them was perhaps intemperate, but he knew what was at stake: 'I may be prejudiced, but I'm pretty sure it won't survive,' he said in 1960, 'I'm prejudiced because if it *does* survive, I know I won't.' [31]

Such was the power and influence of the new movement that Rattigan almost immediately seemed old-fashioned. And from now on, his plays began to receive an almost automatic panning. His first play since *Separate Tables* (1954) was *Variation on a Theme* (1958). But between those dates the critical mood had changed. To make matters worse, there was the widely publicized story that nineteen year-old Shelagh Delaney had written the successful *A Taste of Honey* in two weeks after having seen *Variation on a Theme* and deciding that she could do better. A more sinister aspect of the response was the increasingly open accusation that Rattigan was dishonestly concealing a covert homosexual play within an apparently heterosexual one. The two champions of Osborne's play, Tynan and Hobson, were joined by Gerard Fay in the *Manchester Guardian* and Alan Brien in the *Spectator* to ask 'Are Things What They Seem?' [32]

When he is not being attacked for smuggling furtively homosexual themes into apparently straight plays, Rattigan is also criticized for lacking the courage to 'come clean' about his sexuality, both in his life and in his writing.[33] But neither of these criticisms really hit the mark. On the one hand, it is rather disingenuous to suggest that Rattigan should have 'come out'. The 1950s were a difficult time for homosexual men. The flight to the Soviet Union of Burgess and Maclean in 1951 sparked off a major witch-hunt against homosexuals, especially those in prominent positions. Cecil Beaton and Benjamin Britten were rumoured to be targets.[34] The police greatly stepped up the investigation and entrapment of homosexuals and prosecutions rose dramatically at the end of the forties, reaching a peak in 1953-54. One of their most infamous arrests for importuning, in October 1953, was that of John Gielgud.[35]

But neither is it quite correct to imply that somehow Rattigan's plays are *really* homosexual. This would be to misunderstand the way that homosexuality figured in the forties and early fifties. Wartime London saw a considerable expansion in the number of pubs and bars where homosexual men (and women) could meet. This network sustained a highly sophisticated system of gestural and dress codes, words and phrases that could be used to indicate one's sexual desires, many of them drawn from theatrical slang. But the illegality of any homosexual activity ensured that these codes could never become *too* explicit, *too* clear. Homosexuality, then, was explored and experienced through a series of semi-hidden, semi-open codes of behaviour; the image of the iceberg, with the greater part of its bulk submerged beneath the surface, was frequently employed.[36] And this image is, of course, one of the metaphors often used to describe Rattigan's own playwriting.

Reaction came in the form of a widespread paranoia about the apparent increase in homosexuality. The fifties saw a major drive to seek out, understand, and often 'cure' homosexuality. The impetus of these investigations was to bring the unspeakable and underground activities of, famously, 'Evil Men' into the open, to make it fully visible. The Wolfenden Report of 1957 was, without doubt, a certain kind of liberalizing document in its recommendation that consensual sex between adult men in private be legalized. However the other side of its effect is to reinstate the integrity of those boundaries – private/public, hidden/exposed, homosexual/heterosexual – which homosexuality was broaching. The criticisms of Rattigan are precisely part of this same desire to divide, clarify and expose.

Many of Rattigan's plays were originally conceived with homosexual characters (*French Without Tears*, *The Deep Blue Sea* and *Separate Tables*, for example), which he then changed.[37] But many more of them hint at homosexual experiences and activities: the relationship between Tony and David in *First Episode*, the Major in *Follow my Leader* who is blackmailed over an incident in Baghdad ('After all,' he explains, 'a chap's only human, and it was a deuced hot night –'),[38] the suspiciously polymorphous servicemen of *While the Sun Shines*, Alexander the Great and T. E. Lawrence from *Adventure Story* and *Ross*, Mr Miller in *The Deep Blue Sea* and several others. Furthermore, rumours of Rattigan's own bachelor life circulated fairly widely. As indicated above, Rattigan always placed great trust in the audiences of his plays, and it was the audience which had to decode and reinterpret these plays. His plays cannot be judged by the criterion of 'honesty' and 'explicitness' that obsessed a generation after Osborne. They are plays which negotiate sexual desire through structures of hint, implications and metaphor. As David Rudkin has suggested, 'the craftsmanship of which we hear so much loose talk seems to me to arise from deep psychological necessity, a drive to organize the energy that arises out of his own pain. Not to batten it down but to invest it with some expressive clarity that speaks immediately to people, yet keeps itself hidden'.[39]

The shifts in the dominant view of both homosexuality and the theatre that took place in the fifties account for the brutal decline of Rattigan's career. He continued writing, and while *Ross* (1960) was reasonably well received, his ill-judged musical adaptation of *French Without Tears*, *Joie de Vivre* (1960), was a complete disaster, not assisted by a liberal bout of laryngitis among the cast, and the unexpected insanity of the pianist.[40] It ran for four performances.

During the sixties, Rattigan was himself dogged with ill-health: pneumonia and hepatitis were followed by leukaemia. When his death conspicuously failed to transpire, this last diagnosis was admitted to be incorrect. Despite this, he continued to write, producing the successful television play *Heart to Heart* in 1962, and the stage play *Man and Boy* the following year, which received the same sniping that greeted *Variation on a Theme*. In 1964, he wrote *Nelson – a Portrait in Miniature* for Associated Television, as part of a short season of his plays.

It was at this point that Rattigan decided to leave Britain and live abroad. Partly this decision was taken for reasons of health; but partly Rattigan just seemed no longer to be welcome. Ironically, it was the same charge being levelled at Rattigan that he had faced in the thirties, when the newspapers thundered against the those who had supported the Oxford Union's pacifist motion as 'woolly-minded Communists, practical jokers and sexual indeterminates'.[41] As he confessed in an interview late in his life, 'Overnight almost, we were told we were old-fashioned and effete and corrupt and finished, and . . . I somehow accepted Tynan's verdict and went off to Hollywood to write film scripts'.[42] In 1967 he moved to Bermuda as a tax exile. A stage adaptation of his Nelson play, as *Bequest to the Nation*, had a luke-warm reception.

Rattigan had a bad sixties, but his seventies seemed to indicate a turnaround in his fortunes and reputation. At the end of 1970, a successful production of *The Winslow Boy* was the first of ten years of acclaimed revivals. In 1972, Hampstead Theatre revived *While the Sun Shines* and a year later the Young Vic was praised for its *French Without Tears*. In 1976 and 1977 *The Browning Version* was revived at the King's Head and *Separate Tables* at the Apollo. Rattigan briefly returned to Britain in 1971, pulled partly by his renewed fortune and partly by the fact that he was given a knighthood in the New Year's honours list. Another double bill followed in 1973: *In Praise of Love* comprised the weak *Before Dawn* and the moving tale of emotional concealment and creativity, *After Lydia*. Critical reception was more respectful than usual, although the throwaway farce of the first play detracted from the quality of the second.

Cause Célèbre, commissioned by BBC Radio and others, concerned the Rattenbury case, in which Alma Rattenbury's aged husband was beaten to death by her eighteen year-old lover. Shortly after its radio première, Rattigan was diagnosed with bone cancer. Rattigan's response, having been through the false leukaemia scare in the early sixties, was to greet the news with unruffled elegance, welcoming the opportunity to 'work harder and indulge myself more'.[43] The hard work included a play about the Asquith family and a stage adaptation of *Cause Célèbre*, but, as production difficulties began to arise over the latter, the Asquith play slipped out of Rattigan's grasp. Although very ill, he returned to Britain, and on 4 July 1977, he was taken by limousine from his hospital bed to Her Majesty's Theatre, where he watched his last ever première. A fortnight later he had a car drive him around the West End where two of his plays were then running before boarding the plane for the last time. On 30 November 1977, in Bermuda, he died.

As Michael Billington's perceptive obituary noted, 'his whole work is a sustained assault on English middle class values: fear of emotional commitment, terror in the face of passion, apprehension about sex'.[44] In death, Rattigan began once again to be seen as someone critically opposed to the values with which he had so long been associated, a writer dramatizing dark moments of bleak compassion and aching desire.

Notes

1. Quoted in Rattigan's *Daily Telegraph* obituary (1 December 1977).
2. Michael Darlow and Gillian Hodson. *Terence Rattigan: The Man and His Work*. London and New York: Quartet Books, 1979, p. 26.
3. See, for example, Sheridan Morley. 'Terence Rattigan at 65.' *The Times*. (9 May 1977).
4. Terence Rattigan. Preface. *The Collected Plays of Terence Rattigan: Volume Two*. London: Hamish Hamilton, 1953, p. xv.
5. *Ibid.*, p. viii.
6. *Ibid.*, p. vii.
7. *Ibid.*, p. vii.
8. cf. Sheridan Morley, *op. cit.*
9. Humphrey Carpenter. *OUDS: A Centenary History of the Oxford University Dramatic Society*. With a Prologue by Robert Robinson. Oxford: Oxford University Press, 1985, p. 123.
10. Rattigan may well have reprised this later in life. John Osborne, in his autobiography, recalls a friend showing him a picture of Rattigan performing in an RAF drag show: 'He showed me a photograph of himself with Rattigan, dressed in a *tutu*, carrying a wand, accompanied by a line of aircraftsmen, during which Terry had sung his own show-stopper, "I'm just about the oldest

fairy in the business. I'm quite the oldest fairy that you've ever seen".' John Osborne. *A Better Class of Person: An Autobiography, Volume I 1929-1956*. London: Faber and Faber, 1981, p. 223.

11. Darlow and Hodson *op. cit.*, p. 83.

12. Norman Gwatkin. Letter to Gilbert Miller, 28 July 1938. in: *Follow My Leader*. Lord Chamberlain's Correspondence: LR 1938. [British Library].

13. Richard Huggett. *Binkie Beaumont: Eminence Grise of the West Theatre 1933-1973*. London: Hodder & Stoughton, 1989, p. 308.

14. Terence Rattigan. Preface. *The Collected Plays of Terence Rattigan: Volume One*. London: Hamish Hamilton, 1953, p. xiv.

15. George Bernard Shaw, in: Keith Newman. *Two Hundred and Fifty Times I Saw a Play: or, Authors, Actors and Audiences*. With the facsimile of a comment by Bernard Shaw. Oxford: Pelagos Press, 1944, p. 2.

16. Henry Channon. *Chips: The Diaries of Sir Henry Channon*. Edited by Robert Rhodes James. Harmondsworth: Penguin, 1974, p. 480. Entry for 29 September 1944.

17. Tom Driberg. *Ruling Passions*. London: Jonathan Cape, 1977, p. 186.

18. See, for example, Norman Hart. 'Introducing Terence Rattigan,' *Theatre World*. xxxi, 171. (April 1939). p. 180 or Ruth Jordan. 'Another Adventure Story,' *Woman's Journal*. (August 1949), pp. 31-32.

19. Audrey Williamson. *Theatre of Two Decades*. New York and London: Macmillan, 1951, p. 100.

20. Terence Rattigan. 'Concerning the Play of Ideas,' *New Statesman and Nation*. (4 March 1950), pp. 241-242.

21. Terence Rattigan. 'The Play of Ideas,' *New Statesman and Nation*. (13 May 1950), pp. 545-546. See also Susan Rusinko, 'Rattigan versus Shaw: The 'Drama of Ideas' Debate'. in: *Shaw: The Annual of Bernard Shaw Studies: Volume Two*. Edited by Stanley Weintraub. University Park, Penn: Pennsylvania State University Press, 1982. pp. 171-78.

22. John Elsom writes that Rattigan's plays 'represented establishment writing'. *Post-War British Drama*. Revised Edition. London: Routledge, 1979, p. 33.

23. Terence Rattigan. *Coll. Plays: Vol. Two. op. cit.*, pp. xi-xii.

24. *Ibid.*, p. xii.

25. *Ibid.*, p. xiv.

26. *Ibid.*, p. xvi.

27. *Ibid.*, p. xviii.

28. Opened on 17 September 1960. cf. *Plays and Players*. vii, 11 (November 1960).

29. Quoted in Irving Wardle. *The Theatres of George Devine*. London: Jonathan Cape, 1978, p. 180.

30. John Osborne. *Almost a Gentleman: An Autobiography, Volume II 1955-1966*. London: Faber and Faber, 1991, p. 20.

31. Robert Muller. 'Soul-Searching with Terence Rattigan.' *Daily Mail*. (30 April 1960).

32. The headline of Hobson's review in the *Sunday Times*, 11 May 1958.

33. See, for example, Nicholas de Jongh. *Not in Front of the Audience: Homosexuality on Stage*. London: Routledge, 1992, pp. 55-58.

34. Kathleen Tynan. *The Life of Kenneth Tynan*. Corrected Edition. London: Methuen, 1988, p. 118.

35. Cf. Jeffrey Weeks. *Coming Out: Homosexual Politics in Britain from the Nineteenth Century to the Present*. Revised and Updated Edition. London and New York: Quartet, 1990, p. 58; Peter Wildeblood. *Against the Law*.

London: Weidenfeld and Nicolson, 1955, p. 46. The story of Gielgud's arrest may be found in Huggett, *op. cit.*, pp. 429-431. It was Gielgud's arrest which apparently inspired Rattigan to write the second part of *Separate Tables*, although again, thanks this time to the Lord Chamberlain, Rattigan had to change the Major's offence to a heterosexual one. See Darlow and Hodson, *op. cit.*, p. 228.

36. See, for example, Rodney Garland's novel about homosexual life in London, *The Heart in Exile.* London: W. H. Allen, 1953, p. 104.

37. See note 36; and also 'Rattigan Talks to John Simon,' *Theatre Arts.* 46 (April 1962), p. 24.

38. Terence Rattigan and Anthony Maurice. *Follow my Leader.* Typescript. Lord Chamberlain Play Collection: 1940/2. Box 2506. [British Library].

39. Quoted in Darlow and Hodson, *op. cit.*, p. 15.

40. B. A. Young, *op. cit.*, p. 162.

41. Quoted in Darlow and Hodson, *op. cit.*, p. 56.

42. Quoted in Sheridan Morley, *op. cit.*

43. Darlow and Hodson, *op. cit.*, p. 308.

44. *Guardian.* (2 December 1977).

The Deep Blue Sea

Terence Rattigan described *The Deep Blue Sea* as 'the hardest of my plays to write'.[1] Unlike his contemporaries, Coward and Priestley, who wrote many of their plays in a matter of days, Rattigan usually took at least six months to produce a rehearsal draft. But this play evolved over almost three years, passing through at least six drafts. Yet these struggles were not purely literary; *The Deep Blue Sea* is, in many ways, his most personal work. The idea for the play was cruelly born on 28 February 1949.

In the late 1930s, Rattigan had begun a relationship with a young actor called Kenneth Morgan. He supported Morgan's career by securing him roles as Kenneth Lake in Anthony Asquith's film of *French Without Tears* (1939) and Paul in the unsuccessful *Follow my Leader* (1940). It was, by all accounts, a tempestuous relationship. Despite falling deeply in love with Morgan, Rattigan refused to let him move in, resulting in rows and numerous temporary separations. Their on-off affair appeared finally to have faded out by 1945, as Rattigan began to be wooed by Henry 'Chips' Channon. Yet when this new relationship began to pall, Rattigan's feelings for Morgan flared up again. But the problems were still unresolved, and Morgan, incensed by Rattigan's refusal to break with Channon, finally left him to live with another actor in Camden, North London. Rattigan was unconcerned, convinced that Morgan would, as he had done countless times before, come back to him.

Rattigan's new play for 1949 was *Adventure Story*, a historical drama on an epic scale about the life of Alexander the Great. Featuring Paul Scofield and a lavish production budget, the company were in Liverpool for the last date of their pre-London tour. On 28 February, talking in his suite at the Adelphi Hotel with *Adventure Story*'s director, Peter Glenville, Rattigan was brought a telephone message by the hotel porter. Evidently shattered by its contents, he handed the note to Glenville, instructing him to read and destroy it. The note reported that Kenneth Morgan was dead. Distressed by his new lover's inconstant behaviour, he had taken 'an overdose of sleeping tablets, but when they had failed to kill him he had draped a tea towel over his head and held himself over a small gas ring, usually used to boil a kettle'.[2] It was this which was to inspire Rattigan's most hard-won play. Leaving the hotel later that evening, with Glenville, Rattigan appeared calmer, though distracted. Suddenly he announced, to no one in particular, 'The play will open with the body discovered dead in front of the gas fire.'[3]

This was only the beginning of a long, painful process of writing. Initially, Rattigan had conceived *The Deep Blue Sea* as a one-act play about a successful suicide attempt. Yet, as his ideas developed, and the play grew to full length, he felt that the story required something both more complex and, in a curious way, more bleak. *The Deep Blue Sea* opens, as Rattigan had initially imagined, with a body lying in front of a gas fire; but now it is has become a failed suicide bid. Hester Collyer has left her barrister husband, Sir William Collyer, to live with Freddie Page, an alcoholic fighter pilot from the last war. Injured beyond endurance by his continual failure to return her passion she has tried to commit suicide, and has only failed because the gas meter ran out before she could complete the act. She is discovered by four other residents of the tenement block she lives in: a married couple, Philip and Ann Welch, the landlady, Mrs Elton, and a mysterious ex-doctor, Mr Miller. The play follows Hester through the rest of the day as the consequences of her attempt induce Freddie to leave her, and threaten to push her towards a second suicide attempt.

Rattigan completed a first draft in September 1950 and a second in December. He wrote a third in early 1951, in an upstairs room at the Stag and Hounds pub in Binfield, Berkshire (provided for him by the landlords, Mr and Mrs Newport, to whom he eventually dedicated the play) and a fourth in September. A pre-rehearsal draft was submitted to the Lord Chamberlain, as required by law, on 8 January 1952 and a rehearsal draft a little over two weeks later.[4]

Getting the play into production was not without its difficulties. Rattigan toyed with the idea of a Broadway premiere, and had the film actress Margaret Sullavan in mind. Yet, mindful of the reluctance of American audiences to respond favourably to his work, he decided against it. Rattigan unsuccessfully pursued Peter Brook, then a rising star of London theatre, to direct the play. Alec Guinness refused the part of Miller, Trevor Howard that of Freddie, and Clive Brook the role of Sir William. For the latter part, Rattigan suggested Laurence Olivier, until the play's producer, Hugh 'Binkie' Beaumont of the legendary H. M. Tennent Ltd., discouraged the idea, probably because Olivier, at the St James's Theatre, was running a rival management. Roland Culver was eventually selected for the part, a bold piece of casting as the actor admitted,[5] since his reputation had been forged almost exclusively in light comedy, including the premieres of Rattigan's *French Without Tears* and *Who is Sylvia?*

The casting of Freddie also proved problematic. The director, Frith Banbury, had set his heart on a rugged actor called Jimmy Hanley. But Roland Culver thought his golfing partner, Kenneth More, might be better casting. Rattigan had seen More in Frederick Lonsdale's *The Way Things Go* in Brighton the year before, and so he was invited to audition at the Globe Theatre in front of Rattigan, Banbury, Culver, Peggy Ashcroft (to play Hester) and Beaumont. It was, as More recalled later, 'just about the most horrifying audience you could imagine'.[6] The result was that, despite feeling that Freddie was 'the most certain, cast-iron part I had ever been offered in my life', More responded with an awkward, terrified audition. Nonetheless, a second attempt was arranged, this one in the less formal surroundings of Rattigan's house at 16 Chester Square, London. More recalls Rattigan steering him towards the cocktail cabinet and offering him two large whiskies before the others arrived. His nerves numbed by drink, More gave a pugnacious and confident reading, at the end of which 'he turned to Rattigan with triumph written all over his face and asked: "Howzat?"'.[7] He got the part.

Casting the lead, Hester Collyer, presented the greatest difficulties. Rattigan had wanted Margaret Leighton, though Frith Banbury thought she would find it hard to project the ordinariness that the part demanded.[8] Instead, Beaumont had his sights on Peggy Ashcroft, whose classical training and rich emotional range seemed fitting for the anguished and passionate Hester. In 1932, she had played Juliet in a production at the Oxford University Dramatic Society, though fortunately she had forgotten Rattigan's small but exquisitely inept contribution to the same production.[9] Less fortunately, Ashcroft had been hoping for a comedy from Rattigan and she hated the part. 'I thought she was terribly selfish and cowardly to try and commit suicide just because her lover left her or was being neglectful,' she said. 'I found her so unsympathetic that I said if I feel like that about the heroine, I can't possibly make an audience sympathise with her'.[10] It took a great deal of Beaumont's considerable charm and persuasiveness to suggest that this distance was precisely what the part required. When Ashcroft eventually accepted the role, Binkie considered this his greatest victory.[11]

Her doubts were, however, not entirely quashed. Tennents' custom was to hold a read-through of the play six weeks before rehearsals to allow for redrafting. Banbury and Ashcroft identified several points which needed attention and Banbury proposed some changes over dinner at Chester Square. Rattigan's urbanity hid a deep insecurity, and he immediately called Beaumont, claiming his play was about to be wrecked.[12] For the second time, Beaumont's diplomacy was called on, and in February 1952 rehearsals began on what was now the sixth draft of *The Deep Blue Sea*. An unusually high production budget of £2,500 was allocated to it. The set was designed with a high degree of realism, down to what the programme memorably records as 'gas fittings kindly loaned by the North Thames Gas Board', which, as pieces of product placement go, hardly ranks amongst the most shrewd.

The opening night at the Duchess Theatre was listened to in tense silence, which was broken as the curtain fell by wild cheering. Rattigan's agonized pruning and rewriting were rewarded with a series of reviews praising the rich emotional complexity that emerged from his elliptical and spare dialogue and action: Harold Hobson in the *Sunday Times* described Rattigan as not so much 'a master of direct statement as of suggestion and implication'. Ashcroft's performance was universally praised; Ivor Brown described how her 'gentle gaspings of distress [...] cry as loud as a whole symphony of pain'. The reviewer for *The Sketch* urged, 'Watch her eyes as she listens. This is not mere impersonation. It is, and excitingly, life'. Many agreed with Hobson's judgement that 'it is the best play Mr Rattigan has written'.[13]

Such a view has recently come back into favour, but for a long time the play was written off as little more than soap opera. Yet in amongst the expert plotting, *The Deep Blue Sea* is a much broader, social play, concerned with the pain suffered by those caught between their desires and a society which will not tolerate them. Hester is unusual amongst onstage women of the time in the admitted force of her sexual desires. At a time when, amongst middle-class women, it was customary to play down or scorn the importance of sexual pleasure within marriage, let alone outside it, Hester's actions are bold indeed.[14] And the play is revealed in the first reviews as a talisman of contemporary views of women. Almost universally, even amongst critics who applauded the play, Hester is demonized, pathologised, treated in the critic Anthony

Cookman's words as 'a sick woman rather than a heroine'. The 1950s saw one of the great waves of enthusiasm for hand-me-down psychoanalytic and therapeutic vocabularies. Ivor Brown's review is typical: 'what fretted this unquiet spirit? Was it just boredom? [...] Was it desire for someone to mother? [...] Perhaps she just needs a good slap or a straight talk by a Marriage Guidance Expert'.

Such criticisms may be contrasted with the alternative view that Hester is not really a woman at all. According to Charles Duff a joke circulating around London theatre in the early 1950s was 'I hear Terry Rattigan's written a new play and Kenneth Morgan's to be played by Peggy Ashcroft'.[15] Vivien Leigh's biographer (un)generously ascribes her weak performance in the film adaptation to the play being 'about a homosexual triangle with Hester's feminine gender simply a cloak to appease theatre-goers and censors'.[16] Indeed, one of the persistent rumours surrounding *The Deep Blue Sea* is that the play was originally written about gay men, and later rewritten as one about heterosexuals. The first draft is tantalisingly missing from Rattigan's archive, but a series of comments on it from John Perry, Beaumont's partner, makes no reference to any homosexual content.[17] Furthermore, until December 1958 the Lord Chamberlain would not allow the representation of homosexuals on the stage; it is thus hard to imagine the commercially-minded Rattigan wasting his time writing a play which could never be staged, even at a club theatre.[18] The play's director Frith Banbury has dismissed the idea of a gay first draft as 'absolute rubbish'.[19] While there is no doubt that the play was inspired by Rattigan's relationship with Kenneth Morgan (and also with Channon), and is inflected throughout with his sense of the precarious position of gay men at that time, it is improbable that a 'gay draft' was ever written.

Furthermore, to read the play as secretly homosexual obscures how Rattigan has transformed the story. What is striking, and particularly so for its time, is the play's incisive commentary on gender relationships and performances. This is established in the first moments: as soon as he discovers Hester Collyer's comatose body, Philip Welch's vain attempt to perform with a heroic masculinity is undermined by touches of irony. Philip insists that his wife, Ann, goes to work while he will 'get there as soon as I can' (p. 7). This is in contrast to the fact that he seems to cope the least well with his discovery. He fumbles for the gas tap and panics when he cannot turn it off, leaving Mrs Elton to discover that it isn't actually on. Philip protectively orders his wife not to come into the room, evidently feeling that the scene is one which might upset a woman's delicate sensibility, yet is then 'slightly surprised at his wife's composure' (p. 8). Later in the scene, when he makes the fateful decision to telephone Sir William, the stage

direction tells us, 'He takes Ann's hand and presses it affectionately. He evidently rather enjoys his strong male act and knows
that he is impressing Ann' (p. 15). Later, in Act Three, Philip
makes common cause with Freddie, in the bungled attempt to
return for the bag. Throughout, Philip's attempts at rugged indi-
vidualism are deflated by Hester. He recalls his own infatuation
with a young woman, but his description of how he went off,
alone, to wrestle with his inner demons is wittily written to
suggest the grandiose self-importance of the man, and is equally
wittily deflated:

> PHILIP [...] I went away for a fortnight all by myself - and of
> course I had hell, but gradually things got sort of clearer in
> my mind, and when I got back I was out of the wood.
>
> HESTER. I'm so glad. Where was it you went?
>
> PHILIP. Lyme Regis.
>
> HESTER. A very pretty spot. (p. 83)

Later in the scene, his condescending and fatuously finger-
wagging advice ('you're not going to do anything silly tonight.
You must have learnt your lesson' p. 86), is neatly undermined by
Hester who shows herself, even in her desperation, to be a far
cleverer strategist than her neighbour.

This picture of flat-footed patriarchal brutality is complemented
by the subtle ironies with which Rattigan diagnoses Freddie's
faults. These faults, it should be said, were not always evident to
the first reviewers, one of whom, writing in *The Spectator,* went as
far as to claim that it is not Freddie, but Hester 'who is the cruel
one. Freddie, in his simple, limited way, is at least capable of
considering the situation from her point of view, and even from
her husband's. Hester can only see it from her own'. What this
rather bizarre comment fails to observe is the distance established
between the audience's and Freddie's perception of events. This is
evident from his very first appearance; against the quiet despair of
the opening scene, Freddie's entrance introduces a quite new and
entirely clashing verbal rhythm and vigour. The tight-lipped
propriety of the Welches and Sir William and the monosyllabic
directness of Miller make way for Freddie who bowls ignorantly
into the room in a flurry of staccato slang: 'Hullo, Hes. How's
tricks? I've just done ninety-three down the Great West. Alvis –
smashing job. Jackie Jackson gave me a lift. We gave up the idea
of playing golf. It started to rain. It's pouring down at Sunningdale.
By the way, a bloody great Rolls was just moving off from here as
I came in. I wonder whose it is, do you know?' (p. 35). The sharp
contrast with Hester, whose simple responses are made without
her once turning to meet Freddie's eye, creates a cruelly ironic
effect which distances Freddie from the audience's sympathy.

This is heightened in his scene with Jackie Jackson. Despite Freddie's continual attempt to assert the seriousness of the situation, his inability to comprehend his own part in bringing it about is subtly underscored by Rattigan. Freddie's RAF slang renders his fumbled attempts at self-justification doubly vacuous: 'but it's too bloody silly, old boy – just because I forgot her birthday' (p. 40), 'I tell you, Jackie – it knocked me ruddy flat', 'My God, aren't women the end!' (p. 41), 'the whole thing's too damn' idiotic' (p. 42). His verbal limitations map his emotional limitations, and at one particularly witty moment we see him insist, 'Hell, it's not that I'm not in love with her, of course I am. Always have been and always will. But – well – moderation in all things – that's always been my motto' adding 'Have another?' as he reaches for the depleted whisky bottle (p. 43). These witty and emotionally resonant ironies underline how Freddie's defensive sarcasm remains cruelly inadequate to the force of Hester's passions. 'I was damned if I was going in to Hes and fall down on my knees and say my darling I have grievously sinned in forget-ting your birthday; if I promise you I'll never do it again, will you promise me you'll never gas yourself again' (p. 42).

It is a mixture of irony and restraint that characterises so much of Rattigan's stagecraft, and nowhere more so than here. Yet while restraint is the method, emotional nakedness is the result. During one rehearsal, Peggy Ashcroft reportedly protested to the director, 'I'm not enjoying this: I feel as if I'm walking about with no clothes on'.[20] The edgy calm which is Hester's way of negotiating the space between passion and surveillance creates sharp divisions between text and subtext, becoming more and more divided as the relationship founders. The most striking moment of this is at the end of Act Two, in one of the most emotionally raw and abandoned moments in modern British drama, with Hester crying for her lover to stay for just another night. Hester's urgent attempts to maintain the status quo are displaced onto the care with which she polishes Freddie's shoes. With every word of Freddie's crassly prepared speech, her reserve disintegrates and, as he moves forward to pick up his shoes, Hester's simple line – 'I haven't finished them' (p. 68) – wrenchingly suggests her desperate attempt to hold onto the last symbol of their relationship. And even here, with Hester 'unrestrainedly weeping', Rattigan's compassionate irony has Freddie plead: 'Please don't cry. You don't know what it does to me' (p. 67). Hester's lines, as Freddie leaves the room, demonstrate the depths of her feeling simply because for once she has disregarded etiquette, caring nothing for what can be overheard. Everything that follows in the play takes place decisively after this undignified display of emotional abandon-ment, but suggests also the freedom of thought and action opened up by that grand gesture. It is this scene which makes clear that

the play is as much about Hester and the world as it is about
Hester and Freddie.[21]

Interestingly, successive drafts show the gradual appearance of a
broader structure of male cruelty.[22] In the first three drafts, it was
the bumbling innocent, Jackie Jackson, who returned for the bag.
Only in the fourth draft does Rattigan restructure the act to have
Philip appear. And, tellingly, he now includes the moment where
Ann interrupts Hester and Mrs Elton to say that her husband has
still not returned from his pub crawl with Freddie.[23] She says, 'I
know it's awfully silly of me . . . but I'm not very good at being
left alone' (p. 71). In the 1993 Almeida Theatre production, the
line was followed by an almost imperceptible hesitation, as the
three women of the play exchanged glances, underlining the
fleeting community of feeling between Hester, deserted by her
lover, Ann, neglected and patronised by Philip, and Mrs Elton, left
by her husband to run the building alone. And this moment is not
merely sentimental; it should be seen alongside the careful way in
which Rattigan has placed Hester between her father the
clergyman, her husband the judge, and her lover, the ex-airman;
Hester's sexuality is policed by a repressive triad of church, law
and the army. It is these moments and structures that open a much
broader sexual politics, and give the lie to any simplistic belief
that the play is simply peopled with men in drag.

Nonetheless, there are traces of gay experience running through
The Deep Blue Sea. The set itself strongly captures the continual
fear of exposure felt by so many homosexual men and women.
The room with a communal stairwell right outside the door is
positioned to encourage a constant awareness of surveillance, with
characters perusing each other's letters, exchanging gossip, and
overhearing one another's conversations. As Miller dourly
observes, 'voices carry on the stairs of this house' (p. 75).
Attempted suicide was illegal in the 1950s, like homosexual
activity, which frequently prevented gay men going to the police
to report robbery or blackmail; as Hester remarks to her husband
'I must be careful what I say [...] I'm speaking to a judge' (p. 25).
In this light, the understatement for which Hobson praised *The
Deep Blue Sea* may be seen as a symptom of necessity.

It is important to remember that homosexuality in the 1950s was
never 'open' in the way some critics wish this play to be.
Compelled by the forces of surveillance, crackdown and
entrapment into covertness, gay men often communicated through
codes and signals.[24] Hester recalls how Freddie made his move:
'quite suddenly he put his hand on my arm and said something
very conventional' (p. 59), a scene which, with its conventional
exchange of sexual signals, would have been a familiar one to gay
men in the early 1950s.

Such hints and codes are at play in the presentation of Mr Miller. At least two of the original critics assumed that Miller's offence was to have performed illegal abortions.[25] Yet little is said about his crime, and Mrs Elton's remarks tend rather more to suggest a homosexual offence. She opines: 'what he did wasn't – well – the sort of thing people forgive very easily. Ordinary, normal people, I mean'. A moment later, she ventures: 'It takes all sorts to make a world, after all – doesn't it? There was a couple once in Number Eleven – ' (p. 74). The reference to 'normal people' and the mention of a 'couple' are characteristically fifties clues to Miller's crime being homosexual.[26]

In earlier drafts, it was less ambiguous. In the second, Mrs Elton's comments are plainly not applicable to an abortionist: 'It's not as if it was anything bad. Not really bad – that is [...] I wouldn't call it shocking. More – well – sort of funny, really. (*With sympathy*) Poor Mr Miller. Human nature's a strange thing, I always say'.[27] And in the climactic confrontation between him and Hester he compares Hester's socially intolerable passion to 'my own psychopathic ailment'.[28] Rattigan was not keen to make the offence too clear, and for one draft tried making the offence heterosexual. The discussion now takes a different turn:

HESTER. Won't he ever get back on the register?

MRS ELTON. Oh no, dear, not a hope. Selling morphine and seducing a patient – they won't ever forgive that. Mind you she was taking it before she met him – in fact I think that's why her husband took her to Dr Miller in the first place – and as far as seduction goes, I've no doubt there was quite a bit on the other foot, too. A dope fiend, after all. Still it didn't look good in the papers – there's no denying – and with the woman taking that overdose, which could have been an accident, I grant, still – [29]

In the final drafts, Rattigan moved back to making Miller's a homosexual offence, yet couched in the kind of code most readily picked up by homosexual members of the audience.

The one persistent criticism that this play has received since the premiere is of the ending. Kenneth Tynan, despite describing it as 'the most absorbing new English play for many seasons' and finding the first two acts 'masterly', reported, 'I shall never forgive Mr Rattigan for his last act. It is intolerable: his brilliance lays an ambush for itself, and walks straight into it. If his heroine kills herself, he will merely be repeating the pattern, so he decides to let her live. But he has stated the case for her death so pungently that he cannot argue her out of the impasse without forfeiting our respect. [...] When, finally, she chooses survival, it is for all the wrong reasons'.[30] This same charge, that Rattigan's well-made playwriting instincts had led him to a refusal at the final hurdle, was echoed by Beverley Baxter in the *Evening Standard*, and has been repeated in other more recent commentaries.[31]

Of course, the play *is* well made. Rattigan's sense of structure is acute, but it is also striking how he manages to revivify some of the familiar mechanisms of the well-made play. A classic device of the genre, typified by Victorien Sardou's *A Scrap of Paper* (1861), is the danger that results from letters passing into the wrong hands. The same thing happens here, yet there is a fluidity and subtlety in the way that Rattigan has the suicide note pass from the mantelpiece to the Welches, then into the pocket of Hester's dressing gown, and finally into the hands of Freddie. Rattigan expertly misdirects us, so that we have forgotten about the letter, until Freddie's desire for a cigarette leads him to stumble across it. This becomes the core of a grotesque scene in which Hester returns home to find Freddie reading the letter out to his friend, Jackie Jackson. The same confidence and theatrical economy marks Rattigan's use of the shilling which Freddie cruelly offers Hester, 'Just in case I'm late for dinner' (p. 54), and which lies on the table until Hester picks it up in preparation for her second suicide attempt. Through these devices (and several others: the bracelet, the whisky bottle, Miller's payment), Rattigan not only creates a satisfyingly taut theatrical unity, but reminds us of the dangerous atmosphere in which these characters live, in which everything is charged with meaning, and where objects and actions are constantly scrutinized, judged and battled over.

Yet despite his use of these generic devices, Rattigan's decision not to have Hester kill herself was an explicit *rejection* of the well-made tragic ending that characterises the work of earlier playwrights like Pinero, the author of *The Second Mrs Tanqueray* (1893). As Rattigan explicitly noted of his abandoned tragic ending, 'in a play of full length it seemed merely sentimental – like the suicide of Paula Tanqueray'.[32] It is easy to see why the critics may have felt cheated of their tragic ending; the play takes place over the course of one day, all in the one room, and almost no violent action occurs on stage. This unshowy preservation of the Aristotelian unities perhaps subtly encourages an audience to expect a tragic ending. Yet Tynan, who was so scathing of Rattigan's invented 'Aunt Edna', the middle-aged middle-brow who liked neat endings, was perhaps being not a little Edna-like himself. *The Deep Blue Sea* in tone and structure resembles not so much Pinero as the late Ibsen of *Little Eyolf*, in which an inexorably more sombre tone is deflected by the most minute final uplift, so that the tentative final reconciliation stands alongside the clearest sense of the heights that need to be scaled before it may be realised.

Further, the successive drafts reveal how keen Rattigan was to expunge the traces of melodrama and moralising sentiment that sometimes characterise the well-made tradition in which he is writing. In the early drafts the dialogue occasionally lapses into sententiousness: Miller, for example, was given the line, 'You're as God made you, and if the world calls you names for that reason – well, they're the world's names not God'.[33] By the final draft, such preaching is carefully reserved for characters like Philip, who are given to such pieties as 'if you do think things out honestly, you'll see how awfully petty the whole thing really is – when you get it in perspective. I mean, without trying to be preachy or anything, it is really the spiritual values that count in this life, isn't it?' (p. 83). The play which finally emerged showed less and less confidence in the stability of a spiritual or religious world, giving Hester's anguish an authentically existential edge.

Any traces of melodrama are similarly purged. In the first surviving draft, the third act is dominated by a lengthy discussion between Hester and Sir William, which is interrupted by Freddie, returning to pack his things. As he leaves – telling Hester that he does not know what he will do without her – there is a power cut in the house, and the room is plunged into darkness. Sir William races back in to find Hester slumped in a faint. When she recovers, and the power has been restored (the symbolic significance of which Sir William heavy-handedly remarks upon), she again refuses to go back to her husband. Once he leaves, Hester's suicide is prevented by Mr Miller, who has been told to keep an eye on her by her husband. Miller somehow persuades her from her suicidal course by linking their predicaments and arguing that 'shipwrecked sailors should cling together, I feel, if only for warmth'.[34] With Hester thus convinced, the play ends. The melodrama of the blackout, and the repetitive sequences of static dialogue remain mutely unconvincing as a way of charting Hester's decision to live.

In the third draft, some of the problems have been rectified. The blackout coincides with Hester's second attempted suicide, though this time the chosen method is cutting her wrists with a broken wine glass. But Miller's argument is still purely a matter of persuasion, as he compares Hester to a blade of grass in one of her pictures, and imagines the absurdity of it wishing to rub itself out for being unique.[35] Freddie now returns after this conversation, which has taken place in the semi-darkness, because the lights flicker back on as Freddie leaves. Again, a character points out the symbolic resonance of the moment.[36]

It is only by the fourth draft that Rattigan finds a sure path through Hester's story. The blackout has now become transformed into the subtler device of having Hester put a rolled-up rug on the floor against the door, which partially darkens the room, and then parallelling that with the final moments in which she lights the gas fire, bathing her in an eerily isolating but finally warm glow. Even more striking is the way in which Rattigan changes the confrontation with Miller. Now his persuasion is not a matter of what Hester calls 'just words'. Instead, in what therapists might now call an 'intervention', he squarely confronts her with the unblinking facts: 'Your Freddie has left you. He's never going to come back again. Never in the world. Never' (p. 89). It is an electrifying theatrical moment, which brings Hester's dilemma to a head through a tactic of stark emotional brinkmanship.

Also significant is that Miller's intervention is now of his own volition, and not requested by Sir William. Indeed successive drafts strip away details of his personal life; as well as making his crime more allusive, an early mention of him as a drinker disappears, and with them a series of resentful comments about Mr and Mrs Elton. As the connections and parallels between Freddie, Sir William and Philip and between Hester, Mrs Elton and Ann emerge through the drafts, Miller's isolation becomes more and more sharply focused. The result of this is to give him the kind of mystery that recalls a character like Inspector Goole in J. B. Priestley's *An Inspector Calls* (1945), but here the effect is not supernatural but rather to allow him a connection only with Hester. Further, by responding to none of the speculations indulged in by the other tenants, he becomes another focus for the play of gossip and rumour that circulates in the house.

The fleeting contact achieved between Hester and Miller recalls that between Crocker-Harris and Taplow in *The Browning Version* and Pollock and Sibyl in *Separate Tables*. In each case, the meeting is awkward, emotionally charged, and suggests a momentary recognition of shared experience between outsiders. Despite the wealth and fame that a series of theatrical successes had given him, Rattigan's sexuality gave him an often sidelong and ironic perspective on events. He suggested something of this ambivalent insider/outsider perspective when discussing *The Deep Blue Sea*: 'The play is a study of a woman whom the right-thinking world must consider bad. Her tragedy is that she is herself a part of that right-thinking world, and that no one in it considers her quite as bad as she does herself'.[37] These internal divisions mirror Rattigan's own relation with his source material. In the most conventional reading, Hester is Kenneth Morgan and Sir William is Rattigan. Yet the situation also mirrors an earlier phase in which Hester is Rattigan, Freddie is Morgan and Sir William is 'Chips' Channon. These ambivalences cross gender, class and the relation between self and other, and, while this is still not a *pièce à clef*, perhaps this helped Rattigan to unlock the savage ironies that make the play a broad, rich and incisive analysis of the sexual power structures in which men and women move.

The first production was a huge success, running for well over a year, and reviving Rattigan's reputation after the disappointing

Adventure Story and *Who is Sylvia?* The play also established Kenneth More as a stage actor. Peggy Ashcroft, despite her misgivings, was widely praised; in September she took a break from the production and Celia Johnson briefly replaced her, offering a cooler, though equally moving interpretation. In December, as Ashcroft left to take up a position in the company at the Shakespeare Memorial Theatre, Stratford, Googie Withers took over, offering a strong, if imitative, performance.

The American premiere was less happy. Margaret Sullavan, whom Rattigan may have had in mind when creating Hester, had made her name in Hollywood melodramas and comedies like *Only Yesterday* (1933) and *The Shop Around the Corner* (1940). Her last stage performance had been in John van Druten's *The Voice of the Turtle* in 1943, the year she left acting apparently to concentrate on raising her family. She came out of this nine-year-long semi-retirement to play Hester. Unfortunately, she disliked not only the role, but also both Frith Banbury, who went over to direct the American production, and her new co-star, Jimmy Hanley, who had been turned down for the original London production, and whom Sullavan considered too fat to play her lover. Relations were strained through rehearsals, as Sullavan objected to much of Banbury's direction, and seemed determined to play herself over and above Hester. In London, Ashcroft's profound ability to play subtext had obviated the need for a number of lines, which were then cut. These had to be restored in New York. Rattigan came to dislike her performance: 'either she plays it all out for "pathos", using her famous tearful voice (put on) in which case she is dull and self-pitying, and the play goes down the drain, or she plays it with her own voice and personality, in which case the play equally goes down the drain because the part becomes hard and matter of fact, and you lose patience with Hester, and can't see what all the fuss is about'.[38]

The American critics certainly could not see what the fuss was about. When the production opened at the Morosco Theatre, 5 November 1952, the emotional complexity that was evident in London had melted away leaving what the *Daily News* called 'soap opera' and the *Post* 'magazine fiction'.[39] Nonetheless, Sullavan was applauded and the play completed a respectable run of 132 performances. From there the production began an extensive and lucrative tour, settling eventually in Chicago, at the Blackstone Theatre, on 8 May 1953, with Uta Hagen replacing Sullavan in Hester's role.[40]

There had been talk of a film from the moment the play opened. Various notables were mooted; George Cukor, Max Ophuls and Alfred Hitchcock were considered as directors; Bette Davis, Marlene Dietrich, Greta Garbo, Deborah Kerr and Olivia de Havilland were all tipped to play Hester, before it was eventually offered to Vivien Leigh, in her first role since *A Streetcar Named Desire* (1951). Alexander Korda paid Rattigan £11,500 for the screen rights and first draft, before doing a distribution deal with Twentieth-Century Fox, which handed creative control to them. They appointed the Russian-born director, Anatole Litvak, who had specialised in psychological thrillers, like *The Snake Pit* and *Sorry, Wrong Number* (both 1951). But the film did not work. Litvak's misguided belief that the film should be 'opened out' diminished the claustrophobia of the original play; scenes including Freddie's minor air crash took the tension out of his relationship with Hester. At the pre-shooting conference, Kenneth More, who had retrieved the role of Freddie, exploded, 'We can't start this film. The script is no good [...] There's too much Litvak in it and not enough Rattigan'.[41] But Rattigan stuck loyally behind the director and the film continued its uncertain path. The weaknesses which had developed in the script were unfortunately enhanced by Litvak's choice of the CinemaScope aspect ratio, which projects an image almost two-and-a-half times as wide as it is high, and squandered the emotional intensity and social claustrophobia of the original. Vivien Leigh's performance was further damaged by the 'lack of sexual chemistry between herself and Kenneth More'.[42] Even the presence of Emlyn Williams and Miriam Karlin could not lift the film, which on its release in 1955 was poorly reviewed.

For some years after the premiere, the play remained a staple feature of repertory companies including productions in Nottingham and Cardiff (1953), Manchester and Bromley (1954). But then it disappeared from the repertoire. Partly this was due to the generally sinking reputation which Rattigan suffered in the 1960s. For a long time, people writing on British theatre habitually compared the play unfavourably with John Osborne's *Look Back in Anger*, the play which marked the end of Rattigan's fortunes, as if the two writers were somehow both trying to write the same play.[43] Perhaps some also suspected there might be some truth in the speculation offered by *The Sketch*, who had wondered if without Ashcroft 'the play might move us less'. Either way, few companies felt like challenging the memory of Ashcroft in the role, and even in the minor revival of Rattigan's work in the late seventies, despite some discussion of Jill Bennett or Claire Bloom taking on the role, London saw no revival, and a production in Birmingham, with Honor Blackman, failed to impress. It is perhaps a measure of how faded was the memory of the play that of the two books published in the 1980s about 'Binkie' Beaumont's management, neither one so much as mentions it.[44]

The assumption of the play as a relic from a late but unlamented theatrical era seemed to be confirmed for the critics by a production which opened on 28 October 1981 at the Greenwich

Theatre, the first London revival for almost thirty years. It starred
Clive Francis as Freddie and Dorothy Tutin as Hester. Francis
King in the *Sunday Telegraph* characterised the evening as a 'time
warp', and almost everyone called it 'dated'. Nicholas de Jongh in
The Guardian bemoaned the obtrusive 'mechanics and
organisation of the play with its comic landlady, a struck off
doctor upstairs and air force chums [which] all belong to another
form of theatre'. While some admired Tutin for giving the
performance of a woman, in Coveney's words, trying to cling to
'remembered ecstasy', others found the ending of Act Two
unintentionally comic as Freddie's attempt to escape from Hester's
clutches led the two to tumble farcically over each other.[45]

The production's director, Alan Strachan, tried to revive interest in
the play once again, this time at the Theatre Royal, Haymarket in
1988, with Penelope Keith in the lead. Michael Coveney wrote,
'Miss Keith comes of age as a serious actress in this role, and not
before time. She is magnificent, mixing the desperation of a
woman entering a new life with that of a palpably well-qualified
denizen of the old. Her interpretation is newly definitive and most
skilfully considered'. Yet this was isolated praise. The production
was generally dismissed as ponderous and the play still accused of
being 'dated and seeming glib'. The earlier criticisms of the play's
over-obvious mechanics were promoted by Charles Osborne in the
Daily Telegraph to the charge that it was, if anything, 'rather
poorly constructed and mechanically plotted, with flat dialogue
and too many awkwardly inserted pieces of [...] information'.[46]

It can take an astonishing, revelatory production to force critics
and audiences to shake off the burden of old assumptions and
prior associations. Rattigan's reputation was no higher in 1993
than when he died. *The Deep Blue Sea* had come back in print
after the 1981 Greenwich production, after several years, but still
major revivals were few, and no one had successfully produced the
play in London in over forty years. And then Karel Reisz's
production at the Almeida Theatre, London, reversed Rattigan's
posthumous fortunes, inspired a string of successful revivals, and
placed *The Deep Blue Sea* firmly in the canon of twentieth-
century British drama.

The production stripped the play of its accumulated period
stylings. The cut-glass accents and drably solid box-set which had
encumbered the play for years were rejected. As John Peter wrote
in the *Sunday Times*, 'some of the lines sound banal: you can just
hear them spoken in the placid, tinkling RADA voices of 1950s
film. But [...] spoken as if they had been written yesterday, they
uncover, with brutal irony, suppressed turmoils of emotion and
terrifying depths of complacency'. William Dudley's set was a
shabby room, divided by a partition, through which the bedroom
could be seen with its red linen sheets, hinting at the deeply sexual

dynamics that drive these characters on. The walls themselves were a dark grey-green and constructed from gauze, lit (by Mark Henderson) so as to be semi-transparent. The striking effect of this was to emphasise the way in which the other residents were able to eavesdrop on, and gossip about, their neighbours; but also it softened the 'neatness' of some of the arrivals, by allowing us to see characters approaching before they enter. The whole room was placed at an angle to the audience, suggesting already the disturbed balance of Hester's world.

Wojtek Pszoniak's Mr Miller delighted in the discomfort around him. His measured, Polish accent combined with his down-at-heel shabbiness offered a mischievous dignity which captured both the mystery and the intensity of the man. Linus Roache caught the emotional frustration of Freddie, while his easy manner and physical attractiveness made Hester's desires understandably compelling. But it was Penelope Wilton's Hester which was the greatest revelation. Her performance had a sensuous maturity, which shifted from subtly ironic scorn for the Welches to her excoriating emotional abandonment at the end of the first half. She played both the enormous reserve and dignity that Hester has brought from her former life and the overwhelming sexual desire that had propelled her into her new one, allowing these warring forces to play with a genuinely tragic power across her face, body and speech. In her final moments on stage, left alone and lit by the gas fire to pack Freddie's things, she paused and breathed in the smell of his clothes for a last time, an almost ritualistic moment of farewell, which marked the decisive journey her performance had made through the play.

The production revealed the play as Rattigan's masterpiece. Paul Taylor and Michael Billington compared the play to Racine; Irving Wardle compared it to Greek tragedy. Charles Spencer, in marked contrast to the reviewers of the two productions from the previous decade, reported that 'it is the emotional truth and unsentimental compassion of the writing that again and again strikes home'. And only five years after a reviewer from *What's On* could dismiss the piece as 'insipid as yesterday's dishwater', Michael Billington declared that 'forty years after its premiere, Terence Rattigan's *The Deep Blue Sea* begins to look like a modern classic: as timelessly true as *Phèdre* in its portrait of the inequality of passion'.[47] The production sold out at the Almeida and transferred to the West End, opening at the Apollo on 22 March 1993, and later being adapted for BBC television.

Since 1993, the play has been revived several times, including a highly-regarded production at the Manchester Royal Exchange, in November 1997, directed by Marianne Elliott, with Susan Wooldridge as Hester, and another in January 1999 at the Lyceum Theatre, Edinburgh. A New York revival was mounted in 1998, produced by Roundabout Theatre Company, directed by Mark Lamos, with Blythe Danner and Edward Herrman.

Reviewing the 1997 Manchester production, the *Sunday Times* reviewer noted some potential similarities with *Look Back in Anger*, yet for once the comparisons were flattering to the play, marking a broader change of fortunes for the work of Rattigan and the 'lost' period of theatre history with which he is always associated. In Autumn 1998, the National Theatre asked a number of British theatre workers to nominate the most significant English-language plays of the twentieth century. Few since 1955 would have been surprised to see *Waiting for Godot* at the head of the resulting list; but only ten years ago, to see *The Deep Blue Sea* placed twentieth, and, in the accompanying list of significant playwrights, its author ranked fifteenth, would have been unthinkable. But even this ephemeral tribute said something about the power of the Almeida's production which had boldly rediscovered a towering and brutally bleak meditation on the cruel consequences of one skirmish between sexual desire and social repression.

Notes

1. Quoted in programme note by Christopher Robinson for the 25 May 1988 revival at the Theatre Royal, Haymarket.

2. Geoffrey Wansell. *Terence Rattigan*. London: Fourth Estate, 1995, p. 189.

3. Michael Darlow and Gillian Hodson. *Terence Rattigan: The Man and His Work*. London and New York: Quartet Books, 1979, p. 175.

4. LCP [Lord Chamberlain's Plays, British Library] 1952/3 and LCP 1952/6, 25 January 1952.

5. Roland Culver. *Not Quite a Gentleman*. London: William Kimber, 1979, p. 148.

6. Kenneth More. *Happy Go Lucky: My Life*. London: Robert Hale, 1959, p. 124.

7. Darlow and Hodson, *op. cit.*, p. 198.

8. Charles Duff. *The Lost Summer: The Heyday of the West End Theatre*. London: Nick Hern Books, 1995, p. 129.

9. See page vii.

10. Quoted in Michael Billington. *Peggy Ashcroft*. London: John Murray, 1988, p. 139.

11. Wansell, *op. cit.*, p. 221.

12. Duff, *op. cit.*, pp. 130-131.

13. All reviews, unless otherwise stated, from the Production File for *The Deep Blue Sea*. Duchess Theatre. 6 March 1952, in the Theatre Museum, London.

14. Arthur Marwick. *British Society Since 1945*. Penguin Social History of Britain. Harmondsworth: Penguin, 1990, p. 66.

15. Duff, *op. cit.*, p. 127.

16. Anne Edwards. *Vivien Leigh: A Biography*. W.H. Allen, 1977, p. 204.

17. Wansell, *op. cit.*, p. 218.

18. The Lord Chamberlain traditionally turned a blind eye to club theatres, for which membership had to be obtained, and which were thus notionally private. But *The Deep Blue Sea* as it stands, if performed as a play about gay men, would almost certainly have been prosecuted. The blind eye was not a legal loophole but a matter of tolerance and convention. At least twice in the forties and fifties, the Lord Chamberlain threatened clubs with prosecution. See my *1956 and All That*. London: Routledge, 1999, pp. 201, 205.

19. Duff, *op. cit.*, p. 128.

20. Duff, *op. cit.*, p. 131. Ashcroft reputedly did not change her mind even after the play had become a success, telling a reporter a year later, 'In *The Deep Blue Sea* I just had to suffer every night, twice on matinée days. And don't you dare say I suffered exquisitely. I hated it'. Quoted in Garry O'Connor. *The Secret Woman: A Life of Peggy Ashcroft*. Weidenfeld & Nicolson, 1997, p. 113. Frith Banbury puts this down to the play mirroring aspects of her personal life, though Ashcroft firmly disputed this (cf. Duff, *op. cit.*, p. 131; Billington, *op. cit.*, 140).

21. This moment is used by Neil Bartlett in his wonderfully imagined account of a mid-century homosexual relationship, *Mr Clive & Mr Page*. London: Serpent's Tale, 1996. This novel is studded with shards of *The Deep Blue Sea* and at one point Mr Page, alone in a tenement room, writes in his diary of his fear of isolation: 'Come back. Come back; come back, don't leave me alone tonight, darling, not tonight, please don't leave me alone tonight not again not tonight' (p. 104). See p. 68 of the present edition.

22. The otherwise well-ordered Rattigan archive holds a confusing proliferation of typescript versions of the play. The first draft seems no longer to exist. There is a copy identified as the second draft and dated 22 December 1950; another is dated 7 February 1951 which is the third draft (a further typescript, also marked 'third', turns out to be identical to this, but retyped with correspondingly different page numbers); a further draft is dated September 1951, yet the copy sent to the Lord Chamberlain (Lord Chamberlain's Play Collection [British Library] LCP 1952/3), with the same cover and date, is substantially different. It seems improbable that Rattigan would have worked on a new version after a copy had been sent for licensing, so it seems reasonable to imagine that the Lord Chamberlain's draft is in fact to be dated somewhere around December 1951. There is a further version, resubmitted to the Lord Chamberlain on 25 January 1952, taking in the many changes made after the read through ([British Library] LCP 1952/6). From this we can deduce that the play went through six drafts, which I shall refer to by their dates: first draft (lost, but c. September 1950), second (December 1950), third (February 1951), fourth (September 1951), fifth (December 1951) and the sixth, the draft taken into rehearsal (January 1952). Small changes were also made in preparing the typescript for publication. Perhaps here is the point to record my thanks to Sally Brown, of the British Library, for help tracking down material related to this play.

23. In the December 1951 draft, Ann's lines suggested that Philip had been forced, rather against his will, to accompany Freddie (III-3); these lines are changed to further show the divisions between the men and women.

24. See my *1956 and All That*, *op cit.*, pp. 170-181

25. See Beverley Baxter in the *Evening Standard*, and, surprisingly, T. C. Worsley in the *New Statesman*, Theatre Museum Production File, *op. cit.*

26. Geoffrey Wansell argues that Miller is a portrait of Rattigan's eccentric therapist, Dr Keith Newman, *op. cit.*, p. 223.

27. *The Deep Blue Sea* (draft: September 1950), III-14.

28. *Ibid.*, III-42. Note that homosexuality was still considered a psychopathic disorder by many – including Rattigan – in the 1950s.

29. *The Deep Blue Sea* (draft: September 1951), III-9.

30. Kenneth Tynan. *Tynan on Theatre*. Harmondsworth: Penguin, 1964, pp. 20-21.

31. e.g. Darlow and Hobson, *op. cit.*, p. 202, and B. A Young. *The Rattigan Version: Terence Rattigan and the Theatre of Character*. London: Hamish Hamilton, 1986, who describes the ending as a piece of 'characteristic Rattigan vagueness' (p. 108).

32. Wansell, *op. cit.*, p. 224.

33. *The Deep Blue Sea,* second draft (December 1950), [British Library: Rattigan Archive], p. III-38.

34. *Ibid.*, p. III-47.

35. *The Deep Blue Sea*, third draft (February 1951), [British Library: Rattigan Archive], p. III-38.

36. *Ibid.*, III-46.

37. 'How The Following Plays Came To Be Written', British Library: Rattigan Archive. It is undated, yet possibly the piece was written for the BBC production of the play on 17 March 1974.

38. Quoted in Wansell, *op. cit.*, p. 230.

39. . *ibid.*, p. 231.

40. I am indebted to David Travis and Ginny Bull for information about American productions of *The Deep Blue Sea.*

41. More, *op. cit.*, p. 149.

42. Edwards, *op. cit.*, p. 204.

43. See, for example, Laurence Kitchin. *Mid-Century Drama*. Revised Edition. London: Faber and Faber, 1962, p. 102; Alan Sinfield, ed. *Society and Literature 1945-1970*. London: Methuen, 1983, p. 176; Robert Hewison. *In Anger: Culture in the Cold War 1945-60*. Revised Edition. London: Methuen, 1988, pp. 83-84 and Christopher Innes. *Modern British Drama 1890-1990*. Cambridge: Cambridge University Press, 1992, pp. 90-91.

44. Richard Huggett. *Binkie Beaumont: Eminence Grise of the West End Theatre 1933-1973*. London: Hodder & Stoughton, 1989; Kitty Black. *Upper Circle: A Theatrical Chronicle*. London: Methuen, 1984.

45. Reviews drawn from *London Theatre Record* i, 20 (24 September-7 October 1981), pp. 502- 504.

46. Reviews drawn from *London Theatre Record*, viii, 11 (26 June 1988), pp. 708-711.

47. Reviews drawn from *London Theatre Record*, xiii, 1-2 (1-28 January 1993), pp. 28-30.

List of Rattigan's Produced Plays

Title	British Première	New York Première
First Episode (with Philip Heimann)	"Q" Theatre, Surrey, 11 Sept 1933, trans. Comedy Th. 26 January 1934	Ritz Theatre 17 September 1934
French Without Tears	Criterion Th, 6 Nov 1936	Henry Miller Th, 28 Sept 1937
After the Dance	St James's Th, 21 June 1939	
Follow My Leader (with Anthony Maurice, alias Tony Goldschmidt)	Apollo Th, 16 Jan 1940	
Grey Farm (with Hector Bolitho)		Hudson Th, 3 May 1940
Flare Path	Apollo Th, 13 Aug 1942	Henry Miller Th, 23 Dec 1942
While the Sun Shines	Globe Th, 24 Dec 1943	Lyceum Th, 19 Sept 1944
Love in Idleness	Lyric Th, 20 Dec 1944	Empire Th (as *O Mistress Mine*), 23 Jan 1946
The Winslow Boy	Lyric Th, 23 May 1946	Empire Th, 29 October 1947
Playbill (The Browning Version, Harlequinade)	Phoenix Th, 8 Sept 1948	Coronet Th, 12 October 1949
Adventure Story	St James's Th, 17 March 1949	
A Tale of Two Cities (adapt from Dickens, with John Gielgud)	St Brendan's College Dramatic Scy, Clifton, 23 Jan 1950	
Who is Sylvia?	Criterion Th, 24 Oct 1950	
Final Test (tv)	BBC TV 29 July 1951	

The Deep Blue Sea	Duchess Th, 6 March 1952	Morosco Th, 5 Nov 1952
The Sleeping Prince	Phoenix Th, 5 November 1953	Coronet Th, 1 November 1956
Separate Tables (*Table by the Window*, *Table Number Seven*)	St James's Th, 22 Sept 1954	Music Box Th, 25 Oct 1956
Variation on a Theme	Globe Th, 8 May 1958	
Ross	Theatre Royal, Haymarket, 12 May 1960	Eugene O'Neill Th, 26 Dec 1961
Joie de Vivre (with Robert Stolz, Paul Dehn)	Queen's Th, 14 July 1960	
Heart to Heart (tv)	BBC TV, 6 Dec 1962	
Man and Boy	Queen's Th, 4 Sept 1963	Brooks Atkinson Th, 12 Nov 1963
Ninety Years On (tv)	BBC TV, 29 Nov 1964	
Nelson – a Portrait in Miniature (tv)	Associated Television, 21 March 1966	
All on Her Own (tv) [adapted for stage as *Duologue*]	BBC 2, 25 Sept 1968 King's Head, Feb 1976	
A Bequest to the Nation	Theatre Royal, Haymarket, 23 Sept 1970	
High Summer (tv)	Thames TV, 12 Sept 1972	
In Praise of Love (*After Lydia, Before Dawn*)	Duchess Th, 27 Sept 1973	Morosco Th, 10 Dec 1974
Cause Célèbre (radio)	BBC Radio 4 27 Oct 1975	
Cause Célèbre (stage)	Her Majesty's Th, 4 July 1977	

THE DEEP BLUE SEA

To

MR. AND MRS. NEWPORT

My host and hostess at the Stag and Hounds, Binfield.
With affection and gratitude.

Characters

MRS. ELTON
PHILIP WELCH
ANN WELCH
HESTER COLLYER
MR. MILLER
WILLIAM COLLYER
FREDDIE PAGE
JACKIE JACKSON

Act One   *Morning*
Act Two   *Afternoon*
Act Three   *Evening*

The action passes during the course of a day in September in the sitting-room of a furnished flat in the north-west of London.

The Deep Blue Sea was first produced at the Duchess Theatre, London, on 6 March 1952, with the following cast:

PHILIP WELCH	David Aylmer
MRS. ELTON	Barbara Leake
ANN WELCH	Ann Walford
HESTER COLLYER	Peggy Ashcroft
MR. MILLER	Peter Illing
WILLIAM COLLYER	Roland Culver
FREDDIE PAGE	Kenneth More
JACKIE JACKSON	Raymond Francis

The play directed by Frith Banbury
Setting by Tanya Moiseiwitsch

ACT ONE

Scene: the sitting-room of a furnished flat in the north-west of London. It is a big room for it is on the first floor of a large and gloomy Victorian mansion, converted to flats after World War I, but it has an air of dinginess, even of squalor, heightened by the fact that it has, like its immediate badly-blitzed neighbourhood, so obviously 'come down in the world'.

There is a door backstage right, leading on to the first-floor landing of the house, and another backstage left, leading into the bedroom. Between them is another small door, evidently put in when the house was converted and which gives access to a tiny kitchen.

There is a window right, curtained at the moment, and in the left wall is a fireplace, originally designed for coal, but now occupied by a gas-fire. On the floor in front of this, dimly seen in the darkened room, lies HESTER COLLYER, *with her head, covered by a rug, very close to the unlit stove.*

There is the sound of voices on the landing outside. A young man (PHILIP) *can be heard calling and a woman* (MRS. ELTON) *answering.*

PHILIP (*off*). Mrs. Elton! Mrs. Elton!

MRS. ELTON (*off*). Yes, Mr. Welch?

PHILIP (*off*). I think it's coming from here.

MRS. ELTON (*off*). From Number Three? I'll just come up.

There is a pause, and then another voice (ANN's) *can be heard from farther away.*

ANN (*off*). What's the matter?

PHILIP (*off*). Escape of gas, darling. Don't light a match or anything, will you?

ANN (*off*). Well, it's not us, I know that.

PHILIP (*off*). No, it's in here –

There is a series of knocks on the door.

MRS. ELTON (*off – calling*). Isn't there any answer? Mr.
  Page? . . . Mrs. Page? (*There is no reply. Off.*) It's all right.
  I've got the pass key.

*There is the sound of a key in the lock, and the door opens,
revealing MRS. ELTON on the threshold. She is caretaker-
housekeeper to the flats, and is in the middle fifties. Behind
her is PHILIP WELCH, aged about twenty-four and, from
his clothes, an office worker.*

Phew! It's here all right. They must have left something on.
  Wicked waste – (*She comes into the room.*)

PHILIP. Careful, Mrs. Elton. Put something over your mouth –

MRS. ELTON. Oh, it's not as bad as that. Coming from the
  kitchen I expect –

*She reaches the window, draws the curtains briskly, and
flings up the window.*

Left his cooker on all night, I shouldn't be surprised. Comes
  in late, a bit the worse for you know what, and makes himself a cup of tea – and turns on all the taps in sight. Someone'll blow this whole house up one of these days – that's
  what'll happen –

*While muttering she has been going towards the kitchen
door. She opens it and goes inside. Meanwhile PHILIP has
taken a step or two inside the room, and now sees the
prostrate HESTER by the fire.*

PHILIP. My God! (*He runs up to her; calling urgently.*) Mrs.
  Elton!

MRS. ELTON *emerges from the kitchen.*

MRS. ELTON. It's not in here –

PHILIP. Mrs. Elton! Quick. Get a doctor or someone –

*He raises HESTER's head away from the fire, and pulls the
rug off her.*

MRS. ELTON. Oh heavens!

PHILIP (*fumbling for the gas faucet*). Where does this thing turn off?

MRS. ELTON. Mrs. Page! Mrs. Page! (She *takes* HESTER's *hand*.) She's not dead, is she?

PHILIP. I don't know. I don't think so. (*In a panic.*) This isn't turned off. I can't turn it off.

MRS. ELTON. Here. Let me. It *is* off. (*She turns the faucet both ways.*) It wasn't on.

PHILIP. It must have been.

MRS. ELTON. It's the meter then. It must have switched itself off at the meter.

PHILIP. Help me get her to the window. You take her feet.

MRS. ELTON. Oh the poor thing! Why did she have to go and do it? What's the point in doing a thing like this?

PHILIP *is supporting her shoulders. We see now that she is dressed in a crumpled day dress.* MRS. ELTON *takes her feet and between them they carry her towards the window.*

PHILIP. Let's get her into this chair. Better turn it round to face the window. All right. I've got her.

MRS. ELTON. This'll mean the police. In twenty-three years Mr. Elton and me have never had a speck of trouble in these flats, and now – Mrs. Page – of all people –

PHILIP *and* MRS. ELTON *lower* HESTER *into the chair.* ANN, PHILIP's *young wife, also an office worker, appears on the landing outside.*

ANN (*calling*). Philip? Are you in there?

PHILIP. Yes. Don't come in.

ANN. We'll be late for the office –

PHILIP. You go on. Tell them I'll get there as soon as I can.

ANN. Is anything wrong? (*She comes into the room.*)

PHILIP (*savagely*). I said not to come in.

ANN *sees* HESTER *and runs over to her.*

ANN. Gas?

PHILIP (*slightly surprised at his wife's composure*). Yes.

MRS. ELTON. She's breathing.

PHILIP. Where's the nearest doctor?

MRS. ELTON. Dr. Brown. No – he's on his holiday. I know. Mr. Miller. I'll get him.

ANN. Mr. Miller upstairs, you mean?

MRS. ELTON (*on her way to the door*). Yes.

ANN. But he's not a doctor.

MRS. ELTON *has run out, and we can hear her calling:* 'Mr. Miller! Mr. Miller!' *as she goes upstairs.*

She's hysterical, Philip. Mr. Miller's not a doctor –

PHILIP *has gone back to the gas-fire, while* ANN *stays at the armchair.*

PHILIP. See this? (*He picks up a little empty bottle from the floor.*) Aspirin. Empty.

ANN. Oh Lord!

PHILIP. And here's the glass. (*He picks up a glass.*) She ground them in here. Look.

ANN. She must have wanted to dope herself, before the gas –

PHILIP. The gas was off. The tap was turned on, but the gas was off. It must have run out in the meter –

ANN. Where's her husband?

PHILIP. I don't know. (*He opens the bedroom door and looks inside.*) The bed hasn't been slept in.

ANN. We ought to get hold of him somehow.

PHILIP. Yes, but how?

ANN (*excitedly*). She's opened her eyes.

PHILIP *joins* ANN *at the chair.*

Mrs. Page! Mrs. Page!

HESTER (*speaking in a low, thick murmur, the words barely distinguishable.*) Finished – Freddie – finished –

PHILIP. Mrs. Page – it's all right – everything's all right, now –

HESTER (*with a low moan*). If you – only would – understand – how happy – like sleep – Freddie – sleep – you must understand – forgive bad writing – poor Freddie – poor darling Freddie –

She moans again, as if in a bad dream, and closes her eyes, shaking her head.

ANN. Don't worry, Mrs. Page. You mustn't worry. You're among friends –

MR. MILLER, *unshaven and in a shabby dressing-gown, comes in hurriedly followed by* MRS. ELTON. *He is about forty and when he speaks it is possible to detect a slight German accent. He is carrying a battered instrument case. He goes over to the chair and pushes* ANN *and* PHILIP *rather brusquely out of the way, before kneeling down in front of* HESTER. *With quick deft movements he makes an obviously practised and professional, if cursory, examination.*

ANN. She came to, a moment ago, and talked. She kept on saying Freddie. And something about being happy – like sleep –

PHILIP. And then she said something about bad writing.

ANN. Forgive her bad writing, it was.

PHILIP. I didn't hear forgive. I just heard – bad writing. We found this on the floor.

He hands him the aspirin bottle. MILLER *nods and slips it into his pocket. Then suddenly he slaps* HESTER*'s face hard. She opens her eyes, bewildered.* MILLER *takes the aspirin bottle from his pocket and holds it up before her eyes.*

MILLER. How many?

HESTER closes her eyes. MILLER *slaps her again.*

How many?

HESTER (*quite clearly*). Twelve. (*She closes her eyes again.*)

MILLER (*to* MRS. ELTON). Where's the bedroom?

MRS. ELTON (*hustling to open the door*). In here.

> MILLER *slips his arms underneath* HESTER*'s body and carries her to the door.*

MILLER (*to* MRS. ELTON). Bring my case, would you please.

> *He goes, with his burden, towards the bedroom.* PHILIP *picks up his case.*

> (*As he goes.*) A glass of hot water, please, Mrs. Elton.

> *He goes into the bedroom, followed by* PHILIP.

MRS. ELTON. Yes, straight away.

> *She comes back into the sitting-room, and goes into the kitchen.* PHILIP *emerges from the bedroom.*

PHILIP. Look, darling, hadn't you better get on to the office? It's all right for me, but I don't like the idea of you being late.

ANN. They'll understand. There's never much in on Mondays, and after all a suicide doesn't happen every day.

PHILIP (*with a glance at the bedroom door*). He seems to know his job all right. Let's hope it's just attempted suicide.

ANN. Poor soul. I wonder what made her do it. Freddie – that's her husband, I suppose?

PHILIP. I think so, yes. I've seen his letters downstairs. Frederick Page, Esq.

ANN. I've never liked the look of him.

PHILIP. She said 'poor darling Freddie'. That doesn't sound as if he'd deserted her, or anything.

ANN. Then where is he?

PHILIP. Husbands do, you know, occasionally go off on business without taking their wives.

MRS. ELTON *comes out of the kitchen with a glass of warm water. She crosses to the bedroom door, knocks, and goes in.*

ANN. I wish we could help, somehow.

She is looking at the fireplace and notices something. She goes quickly over and takes a letter off the mantelpiece.

ANN. Yes. Of course.

PHILIP. What?

ANN (*holding up the letter*). Suicide note. We should have thought of that.

PHILIP. Who's it addressed to?

ANN (*reading*). 'Freddie'. It's in pencil – very faint.

PHILIP. 'Forgive my bad writing'. I expect that's in it. She'd probably taken the aspirin.

ANN. Should we open it?

PHILIP. No. It may be wanted by the police.

ANN. The police? Oh dear.

PHILIP (*unhappily*). I suppose we ought to ring them up.

She puts it back quickly on the mantelpiece.

ANN. It's a sordid business, isn't it, a suicide? I wonder if they think of that when they do it – police and coroners and things. I suppose we'll have to give evidence.

PHILIP. If there's an inquest, yes. But let's pray it doesn't come to that.

ANN. Attempted suicide is a crime, anyway, isn't it? People get jailed for it, don't they?

PHILIP. Yes.

ANN. Well, then, you mustn't ring up the police. Not yet anyway.

PHILIP. We ought to get in touch with somebody, though. I wish to God her husband would come. That letter proves he hadn't deserted her. She expected him. Put it back exactly where you found it, darling.

ANN. I did.

PHILIP. No. Only a bit of it was showing. It was half behind that clock –

ANN *gingerly puts the letter in the indicated position.* MRS. ELTON *comes out of the bedroom.*

(*To* MRS. ELTON.) How is she?

MRS. ELTON. He didn't say, but she's looking better. He's given her an injection of something. That made her sick. I've got to make some black coffee.

She goes back into the kitchen, PHILIP *follows her to the door.*

(*Off.*) There's some here ready. I'll just need to warm it up –

PHILIP (*calling after her*). Mrs. Elton, we both think we ought to get hold of Mr. Page. Have you any idea where he might be?

MRS. ELTON *appears at the door.*

MRS. ELTON. No. I can't say I have.

PHILIP. Does he go away often?

MRS. ELTON. Now and then. Not for more than a night usually –

PHILIP. Where does he work?

MRS. ELTON. I don't know that he does work – not regularly that is. He's often here all day, I know that. I believe he's something to do with aeroplanes – or used to be, anyway.

PHILIP. Selling them?

MRS. ELTON. No. Flying them, I think. Test pilot – isn't that what they call it?

PHILIP. Yes. You don't know for which company?

MRS. ELTON. No. Besides, I tell you, I don't think he's doing it any more –

She goes back into the kitchen.

· ANN. She must have some relations in London we could get hold of.

PHILIP. Yes. (*He goes to the kitchen door again. Calling.*) Mrs. Elton. Do you know if Mrs. Page has any relations in London?

MRS. ELTON *reappears and comes in, leaving the kitchen door open.*

MRS. ELTON. No. I can't say I do.

PHILIP. Can you think of any particular friend then? Haven't you ever heard her talk about anybody?

MRS. ELTON. No. Always kept herself very much to herself, Mrs. Page.

ANN. She must have had visitors –

MRS. ELTON. Hardly at all, and they always asked for him – not for her.

PHILIP. What were their names?

MRS. ELTON. I can't remember.

PHILIP. Do try and help, Mrs. Elton. This is desperately important.

MRS. ELTON. I'm sorry, Mr. Welch. It's the shock.

PHILIP. Yes, yes of course. But now look. Think hard. Don't you know of anyone connected with Mrs. Page we might get into touch with?

ANN. Solicitor – bank manager –

Pause. MRS. ELTON *frowns in concentration.*

MRS. ELTON (*at length.*) There *is* her husband, of course –

PHILIP (*with a hopeless gesture*). I know – but we haven't an idea where he is –

MRS. ELTON. I didn't mean – (*She looks alarmed.*) No, I can't think of anyone. (*She turns to go back into the kitchen.*)

ANN (*sharply*). Mrs. Elton. What did you mean by 'There *is* her husband'?

MRS. ELTON *turns slowly.*

Isn't Mr. Page her husband?

Pause.

PHILIP. What's her real name?

MRS. ELTON. I haven't said anything.

PHILIP. Look, Mrs. Elton. If the police come, it'll all have to come out anyway. You don't need to tell us anything you don't want to; but I do think that if you know her real husband you ought to ring him up and tell him what's happened.

MRS. ELTON. I don't know her real husband. And what I do know I promised faithfully I'd never tell a living soul. It was all because I picked up her ration book one day, and then she told me straight out quite simply all about it – how she hadn't been able to get herself a divorce. Poor lamb – she thought Mr. Elton would turn her out. I found her that evening packing her things. I told her not to be silly. As if I'd tell Mr. Elton a thing like that. It's none of his business, or mine, or anyone else's, come to that.

She goes into the kitchen. PHILIP *and* ANN *exchange a glance.*

ANN. I'm sure I'm right now, Philip. This man Page has deserted her, and she had no one to turn to. She's probably quarrelled with her family, and her friends have dropped her, most likely –

MRS. ELTON *emerges with a cup and saucer on a tray.*

MRS. ELTON. So you think I ought to tell her husband about this?

PHILIP. Well, yes, Mrs. Elton. It seems to me the only thing to do.

MRS. ELTON. All right. You do it. I wouldn't know how. Her name is Collyer – (*Spelling it.*) C-O-L-L-Y-E-R, and her husband's name's in the papers quite often. She showed me once. They call him Mr. Justice Collyer – so I suppose he's a judge.

ANN. Sir William Collyer.

MRS. ELTON. That's right. Sir William Collyer.

She goes into the bedroom.

PHILIP (*awed*). Gosh!

ANN. Do you think you dare, Philip?

PHILIP. I don't see why not.

He has grasped a telephone book and is looking through it.

ANN (*in a panic*). Whatever you do, don't tell him you work at the Home Office.

PHILIP (*he looks at his watch*). Quarter past nine. We ought to get him at his home. Here we are – Collyer – William – there are two, but one's in Chiswick. Eaton Square – that's the one. (*He dials a number.*)

ANN *waits by his side.*

(*At length.*) Hullo. Could I speak to Sir William Collyer, please? . . . No, I'd rather not give my name. Just tell him that it's very urgent indeed, and that it concerns his wife . . . His wife . . . Yes. I'll wait.

He takes ANN*'s hand and presses it affectionately. He is evidently rather enjoying his strong male act and knows that he is impressing* ANN.

Hullo! Sir William Collyer? I'm afraid I have some serious news for you. Your wife has been concerned in – an accident . . . It's rather difficult to tell you that on the telephone . . . Well, if you insist. Gas poisoning, and an overdose of drugs . . . No, but very ill . . . No. She doesn't know I'm telephoning . . . He's not here . . . 27 Weybridge Villas, Ladbroke Grove . . . Yes. Flat Number Three, first floor. . . . You'll find the front-door open. Yes. There's a doctor – that's to say, she's being given medical attention now. (*He rings off.*) He's coming round at once.

ANN. Did he seem upset?

PHILIP. It was rather difficult to tell. He asked if Page was here.

MRS. ELTON *comes out of the bedroom.*

I've rung him up, Mrs. Elton. He's coming round.

MRS. ELTON (*slowly*). I only hope we've done the right thing.

ANN. I think we have.

PHILIP. How is she?

MRS. ELTON. Sitting up now. Drank her coffee quite peacefully. Of course – still very weak.

ANN. Don't you think we ought to get her a proper doctor?

MRS. ELTON. I've got far more faith in Mr. Miller than in any proper doctor thank you very much. He's done a sight more for Mr. Elton than any of those Harley Street specialists ever did – five guineas or no five guineas.

PHILIP. How is Mr. Elton?

MRS. ELTON. Well, he'd be much better if it weren't for this damp weather. Shocking for arthritis, it's been. I've been fixing his pillows all night long. (*She goes to the door.*) Well, I've got to give Number Six his tea and I haven't started on my hall yet. Give me a shout if I'm wanted, will you.

PHILIP *and* ANN *nod.* MILLER *comes out of the bedroom.*

Will you be wanting me for anything more?

MILLER. No, Mrs. Elton.

MRS. ELTON. I'll leave this door on the latch.

She goes out.

MILLER (*to* PHILIP). Have you a cigarette?

PHILIP. Yes, indeed. (*He brings out a small packet.* MILLER *takes a cigarette and lights it.*) My name is Welch. I live upstairs in Number Five. This is my wife.

MILLER *nods to* ANN.

MILLER. Are you friends of hers?

ANN. No. My husband found Mrs. Page this morning and we were just waiting around to see if there's anything we can do.

MILLER. There is nothing you can do.

ANN (*appalled*). You don't mean she's dying?

MILLER (*smiling*). On the contrary.

PHILIP. She'll recover?

MILLER. Sixty grains of aspirin are hardly enough to kill a healthy child, and the symptoms of gas poisoning are very slight –

PHILIP. That's because the gas gave out at the meter.

MILLER. Yes. She couldn't have bungled it worse, could she? I must go back to my breakfast and I'm sure there is no reason whatever for your staying here any longer. Good morning.

ANN. But is she really all right?

MILLER. I've told you. After twenty-four hours in bed she will be completely recovered.

ANN. Yes – her body. But what about her mind?

MILLER (*Amused*). You make that distinction? Her mind is perfectly sound. There is no trace whatever of any psychotic symptoms which might justify a certificate of insanity.

ANN. Yes – but she did try to kill herself, didn't she?

MILLER. It would seem so.

ANN. Well – what made her do that?

MILLER (*after a slight pause*). She wanted to die, I suppose.

PHILIP. But mightn't she try to do it again, Doctor?

MILLER. I'm not a doctor.

PHILIP. No. Don't you think she might try to do it again?

MILLER. I'm not a prophet either. In fact I make a fairly respectable living out of other people's pretensions to prophecy. Still, if you want me to be a punter for once, I would say that she probably will try again, and try again very soon.

ANN (*indignantly*). But isn't there anything we can do about it?

MILLER. (*gently shaking his head*). No.

He goes out.

PHILIP. Well, there's a callous swine, if you like.

ANN. He's phoney, that man. I'm certain he is. He was just trying to impress us with all that stuff about psychoses and things. Of course she's ill. Of course she needs looking after.

The bedroom door opens and HESTER *comes out. She is in a dressing-gown, but has tidied her hair, and put on make-up. Now that we see her under more normal circumstances we find that she is in the middle thirties with a thoughtful, remote face that has no pretensions to great beauty.*

Oh! Should you be out of bed?

HESTER. I came for a cigarette. There was a packet here last night, I think.

PHILIP. Have one of these. (*He extends his packet.*)

HESTER. No, I won't smoke yours. I know I brought a packet in with me. (*She searches on the table.*) Ah yes. Here they are.

She takes a cigarette. PHILIP *lights it for her.*

Thank you so much. You're Mr. Welch, aren't you? We met downstairs once, do you remember?

PHILIP. Yes, that's right.

HESTER. And is this Mrs. Welch?

ANN. Yes.

HESTER. How do you do? Do you mind if I sit down? I'm still feeling a little strange. (*She sits down.*)

ANN. Don't you think you ought to go back to bed?

HESTER. Oh no. I feel much better sitting up, thank you.

PHILIP. You've been very ill, you know.

HESTER. Oh no. Just a bit dopey, that's all. Idiotic accident,
   wasn't it? I'm terribly sorry for all the trouble I've caused –

PHILIP *and* ANN (*murmuring*). That's quite all right.

HESTER. I don't know how it could possibly have happened.
   I'd been out to a cinema, by myself, and I came back here.
   I remember thinking it was a bit chilly and I turned on the
   gas-fire to light it, and after that, as they say in novels,
   I knew no more. I couldn't find the matches, I suppose,
   and the fumes must have put me out –

ANN (*rather crossly*). It was lucky for you that you didn't put
   a shilling in the meter first.

HESTER. The meter?

PHILIP. Yes. The gas cut off automatically.

HESTER. Oh. That's what happened, is it? (*After a pause.*)
   Yes. That was lucky. (*She leans back in the chair and closes
   her eyes.*)

ANN. Are you sure you're feeling all right?

HESTER (*opening her eyes*). Perfectly all right, thank you.

ANN. Don't you think you ought to see a proper doctor?

HESTER. Haven't I just seen a proper doctor?

ANN. He's only an amateur. Bookmaker's clerk or something.

HESTER. A strange hobby for a bookmaker's clerk. He seemed
   very efficient. Horribly efficient. Look, I'm sure I'm
   keeping you both, and there's really no need to stay. It's
   been very kind of you.

PHILIP. Well – (*He looks to* ANN *for support.*) The fact is
   I have something to tell you.

   HESTER*'s eyes are wandering over the room.* ANN *is
   watching her.*

ANN. Are you looking for something?

HESTER. Yes. I think I left a letter lying around somewhere.

   ANN *goes to the mantelpiece and takes the letter from
   behind the clock.*

ANN. Is this it? (*She hands it to her.*)

HESTER (*gazing at it casually*). Yes. That's the one.

She slips it into her dressing-gown pocket.

(*Politely to* PHILIP.) You were going to tell me something?

PHILIP. You may be very angry with me.

HESTER. I hope not.

PHILIP. I hope not, too. When we found you this morning you seemed – very ill – almost at death's door, in fact –

HESTER *glances at the fireplace, but says nothing.* PHILIP *continues after a pause.*

Mr. Page was away, and we didn't know where to get hold of him –

HESTER. You should have asked me. He's at the King's Head Hotel, at Sunningdale.

ANN (*quickly*). Are you expecting him back this morning?

HESTER. No, I think he's playing golf. (*Smiling.*) I'm a golf widow, you know, Mrs. Welch. Every weekend I'm deserted. It's shocking. (*To* PHILIP.) Go on.

PHILIP (*desperately*). Well, I felt it my duty to get in touch with someone. We didn't know where your parents lived –

HESTER. They're both dead anyway.

PHILIP. Or any of your friends.

HESTER *nods.*

So I'm afraid I took it on myself to ring up – Sir William Collyer.

There is a pause. HESTER *gets up and puts out her cigarette.*

HESTER. What did you tell him?

PHILIP. That there'd been an accident.

HESTER. Did you give him this address?

PHILIP. Yes. He's coming round.

HESTER. How soon?

PHILIP. He said, at once.

>   HESTER *looks at the bedroom door, as if meditating whether she has time for flight.*

>   I'm sorry if I've done wrong. I couldn't know, you see.

HESTER. No, you couldn't.

ANN (*loyally*). It was mainly my responsibility, Lady Collyer. It was I who told Philip he ought to ring up.

HESTER. Yes, I see. Do you mind not using that name?

ANN. I'm sorry.

HESTER. It was Mrs. Elton who told you?

PHILIP. She slipped it out by accident. I may say your secret is absolutely safe with both Ann and myself.

HESTER (*with a faint smile*). My guilty secret? That's very kind of you both.

PHILIP (*stiffly*). Well, I think we must be going. Come along, Ann.

>   ANN *and* PHILIP *go to the door.*

HESTER (*with contrition*). Goodbye. You've been very kind, and I'm grateful.

PHILIP. There's no need. Let me know if there's anything I can do, won't you?

HESTER. There is something you can do. Don't breathe a word of this stupid – accident – to anyone – to anyone else, that is.

PHILIP. I won't.

HESTER. Do you know my – do you know Freddie Page?

PHILIP. No.

HESTER. If ever you should meet him you will, above all, be particularly careful not to mention anything of this to him, won't you? It might – it might alarm him – quite unnecessarily.

ANN. We won't say a word – either of us.

HESTER. Thank you. Goodbye.

PHILIP. Goodbye.

ANN. Goodbye – Mrs. Page.

She follows PHILIP *out.* HESTER, *after a moment, goes out on to the landing.*

HESTER (*calling*). Mrs. Elton! Mrs. Elton!

MRS. ELTON (*off*). Coming, dear. (*She comes in.*) You're up. I'm sure you shouldn't be.

HESTER (*abruptly*). Mrs. Elton, if Sir William Collyer comes, I don't want to see him.

MRS. ELTON. I'm sorry about that. They got it out of me –

HESTER. Yes, I know.

MRS. ELTON. What shall I tell him?

HESTER. Anything you like – provided I don't have to see him.

MRS. ELTON. Yes, dear. I understand. Would you like me to make you some more coffee?

HESTER. No, thank you, Mrs. Elton. There's nothing I want at all.

MRS. ELTON. When's Mr. Page coming home?

HESTER. I don't know. Some time this evening, I expect.

MRS. ELTON. I'll come and sit with you, if you like, until then. I've just got to finish my work –

HESTER. It's very kind of you, Mrs. Elton, but I shall be perfectly all right alone.

MRS. ELTON (*doubtfully*). Will you, dear? Are you sure?

HESTER. Yes. You can trust me.

MRS. ELTON. Oh, I didn't mean that –

HESTER (*gently*). Didn't you?

MRS. ELTON (*angrily*). Whatever possessed you to do a dreadful thing like that?

Pause.

HESTER (*lying back with her eyes closed*). The devil I suppose.

MRS. ELTON. I should just think it was. Are you a Catholic?

HESTER (*sleepily*). No. I didn't mean that kind of devil. Or is it the same kind? Anyway when you're between any kind of devil and the deep blue sea, the deep blue sea sometimes looks very inviting. It did last night.

MRS. ELTON. I can't make you out. You're not a wicked woman – and yet what you did last night was wicked – wicked and cruel. Now supposing it had been Mr. Page and not you that we'd found lying there this morning, how would *you* have felt?

HESTER. Very, very surprised.

MRS. ELTON. Nothing more?

HESTER. Oh yes. A lot more. A whole universe more. (*With a faint smile.*) He's not lying there. He's playing golf.

Pause. MRS. ELTON *is looking at her, puzzled.*

And when he comes back from golf, he must know nothing of what happened last night. Do you understand, Mrs. Elton? Nothing.

MRS. ELTON. If that's the way you want it.

HESTER. That's the way I want it.

Pause.

MRS. ELTON. It's not money, is it, dear?

HESTER. No. It's not money.

MRS. ELTON. Because if it is, I was going to say – about this flat –

HESTER (*quickly interrupting*). It's very kind of you, Mrs. Elton, and I'm deeply grateful. But I couldn't accept it. I know we owe you a month's rent – but it will be paid, I promise you, in a day or two – As a matter of fact I've got someone who's very interested in those two pictures there. (*She points to two pictures on the wall.*)

MRS. ELTON. Oh yes. Very nice. (*Pointing to one.*) That's a pier, isn't it?

HESTER. Weymouth Pier.

MRS. ELTON (*politely*). Oh yes. You can tell at once. Very clever. How much would you get for a thing like that?

HESTER. Well – for the two I'm asking twenty-five pounds.

MRS. ELTON. Are you, really? Well, I never. (*After a slight pause.*) Excuse me asking you, won't you – but is Mr. Page in a job just now?

HESTER. Not exactly. Not at the moment. But – he has interests in the city – you know.

MRS. ELTON (*who has evidently heard this one before*). Oh yes? Well, perhaps he'll get himself something steady soon. It shouldn't be too hard these days –

She moves towards the door, then stops at the sound of a loud knock on the door. MRS. ELTON *waves* HESTER *out of sight of the door and goes to open it.* COLLYER – *a forceful-looking figure in the middle forties, dressed in short morning coat and striped trousers – stands on the threshold.*

COLLYER. Mrs. Page?

MRS. ELTON. I'm sorry, sir – you can't come in. Mrs. Page is too ill to be bothered –

COLLYER *brushes her impatiently aside and walks into the room. He sees* HESTER *at once. They stare at each other without speaking.* MRS. ELTON *flutters helplessly between them.*

COLLYER (*to* HESTER). Tell her to go.

HESTER. It's all right, Mrs. Elton. Thank you.

MRS. ELTON *shrugs her shoulders and departs.* COLLYER *and* HESTER *still stare at each other.* HESTER*'s alarm, now that she is finally confronted with her husband, seems to have dissipated.*

COLLYER. Are you all right?

HESTER. Quite all right.

COLLYER. What happened?

HESTER. How much did that boy tell you on the telephone?

COLLYER. Enough to spare you the necessity of lying to me.

HESTER. I must be careful what I say. Attempted suicide is a crime, isn't it?

COLLYER. Yes.

HESTER. And I'm speaking to a judge.

COLLYER. You're speaking to your husband.

HESTER. Shall we say, *crise de nerfs?*

COLLYER. Nonsense. You're as sane a person as any in the world.

HESTER. Perhaps I've changed since I left you, Bill. No, I'd better not say that. It might give you an opportunity of saying I told you so.

COLLYER. You misjudge me.

HESTER. Misjudge a judge? Isn't that *lèse-majesté?*

There is a pause while HESTER *stares at him.*

COLLYER. Why didn't you let me know you were in London?

HESTER. The last time I saw you you said you never wanted to hear from me again.

COLLYER. The last time I saw you I didn't know what I was saying. How long have you been back from Canada?

HESTER. Oh, three or four months now. Freddie lost his job you see – that's to say he gave it up – it wasn't a very good one – and we neither of us liked Ottawa very much –

COLLYER. Why didn't you answer my letter?

HESTER. I never got a letter.

COLLYER. Oh, didn't you? I addressed it to the aircraft firm in Ottawa, and put 'please forward'.

HESTER. Oh. We left rather hurriedly, and I forgot to leave a forwarding address. What did you say in the letter, Bill?

COLLYER. Just that you could have your divorce if you still wanted it.

HESTER. Oh!

COLLYER. Not getting a reply I'm afraid I've taken no steps.

HESTER. No. That was generous of you, Bill. Still I should have thought what you said before about the scandal would be even more operative now that you're a judge.

COLLYER. What I said before was exaggerated. I wanted to put every difficulty in your way that I possibly could.

HESTER. Sit down, Bill, now you're here. It's nice to see you again. Have a cigarette?

COLLYER (*ignoring the proffered packet*). No thank you. (*He lights her cigarette.*) Has he deserted you?

HESTER. He's playing golf at Sunningdale. He plays there a lot these days. I wonder you haven't run into him.

COLLYER. I haven't ever been to Sunningdale since –

HESTER. You still feel so strongly?

COLLYER. You know I do.

HESTER. I know you did – but after all this time? I suppose ten months isn't very long. I keep thinking it's so much longer.

COLLYER. Has it seemed so much longer?

HESTER (*quietly*). Yes, Bill. Almost a lifetime.

Pause.

COLLYER. Is he being unfaithful to you?

HESTER. No.

COLLYER. He still loves you?

HESTER (*after a slight pause*). As much as he did ten months ago.

COLLYER. And you still love him?

HESTER. Yes, Bill. I still love him.

COLLYER. Is it money?

HESTER. No. It isn't money.

COLLYER. He's still got a job?

HESTER. Not as a test pilot. He gave that up some time ago. He's – he's working in the city now, you know.

COLLYER. In a job in which they allow him to play golf on Mondays?

HESTER. Well – it's a sort of free-lance job, you see.

COLLYER. Yes. I see. What salary –

HESTER. You're on the wrong track, Bill. All right. We do owe a month's rent, but money had nothing to do with it.

COLLYER. What was it then?

HESTER. Bill, I'm not in the witness box and you'll never get me to confess that I had any reason for trying to kill myself last night. Any logical reason, that is.

COLLYER. But you did try to kill yourself?

HESTER. While the balance of my mind was temporarily disturbed. Isn't that the legal phrase?

COLLYER. What was it that disturbed the balance of your mind?

HESTER. Oh dear, oh dear, I don't know. A great tidal wave of illogical emotions.

COLLYER. Can you give a name to those emotions?

HESTER. Yes, I suppose so. Anger, hatred and shame – in about equal parts I think.

COLLYER. Anger – at Page?

HESTER. Yes.

COLLYER. And hatred – ?

HESTER. Of myself, of course. (*Pause.*) Shame at being alive.

COLLYER. I see.

HESTER. Do you?

COLLYER. No, I suppose I don't. Can I do anything to help?

HESTER. No, Bill. Nobody can.

COLLYER. Well – at least I've found you again.

HESTER. Were you looking so very hard?

COLLYER. No. You see, rather foolishly I thought my indifference would hurt your vanity.

HESTER only smiles in reply.

You must understand that I'm very inexperienced in matters of this kind.

HESTER (*gently*). So am I, Bill. Almost as inexperienced as yourself.

She touches his arm sympathetically. He takes hold of a bracelet she is wearing.

COLLYER. I'm glad you still wear it.

HESTER. What? (*Remembering with an effort.*) Oh yes, of course. An anniversary present, wasn't it?

COLLYER. Our seventh.

HESTER (*awkwardly*). It was a good party we gave that night. All our nicest friends, weren't they?

COLLYER nods.

I read Sibyl's new book. I didn't think it was as good as her last. Tell me, is David very pompous now he's Solicitor-General?

COLLYER. No. Not very.

HESTER. Is Alice still as gay as ever? (COLLYER *nods.*) Oh dear. (*She sighs nostalgically.*) Didn't I make a speech that night?

COLLYER. Yes. Old Lord Marsden was wildly impressed.

HESTER. That's what comes of being a clergyman's daughter. I could always impress your erudite friends, when put to it. I only wish I were as good with Freddie's friends.

COLLYER. Aren't you?

HESTER. Oh no. On pub crawls I'm a terrible fish out of water.

COLLYER. Pub crawls?

HESTER. Oh, you needn't be shocked. There's nothing in the the world more respectable than pub crawls. More respectable or more unspeakably dreary.

Pause.

COLLYER. Hester –

HESTER. Yes?

COLLYER. It doesn't matter. The question I was going to ask you is too big to put into a single sentence.

HESTER (*slowly*). Perhaps the answer could be put into a single word.

COLLYER. We might disagree on the choice of that word.

HESTER. I don't expect so. There are polite words and impolite words. They all add up to the same emotion. (*Pointing to a picture.*) That's my latest.

COLLYER. Very nice. What were you angry with Page about?

HESTER. Oh, lots of things. Always the same things.

COLLYER. What?

HESTER. That word we were talking about just now. Shall we call it love? It saves a lot of trouble.

COLLYER. You said just now his feelings for you hadn't changed.

HESTER. They haven't, Bill. They couldn't, you see. Zero minus zero is still zero.

Pause. COLLYER *pushes her away from him to look into her eyes.*

COLLYER. How long have you known this?

HESTER. From the beginning.

COLLYER. But you told me –

HESTER. I don't know what I told you, Bill. If I lied, I'm sorry. You must blame my conventional upbringing. You see I was brought up to think that in a case of this kind it's more proper for it to be the man who does the loving.

Pause.

COLLYER. But how, in the name of reason, could you have gone on loving a man who, by your own confession, can give you nothing in return?

HESTER. Oh, but he can give me something in return, and even does, from time to time.

COLLYER. What?

HESTER. Himself.

COLLYER *stares at her. There is a pause.*

COLLYER. Perhaps you're right, Hester. Perhaps there is no one who can help you.

HESTER (*mockingly*). Except myself, you were going to say.

COLLYER. Yes, I was.

HESTER. I thought you were. (*She turns to the picture.*) It's rather good, I think, don't you?

COLLYER. Yes. Are you selling it?

HESTER. Oh yes, I suppose so – if anyone will buy it.

COLLYER. I'll buy it.

HESTER (*with a hint of anger*). No, you won't.

COLLYER. Why not?

HESTER. Because I don't want you to – that's why not.

COLLYER. Hester – don't be childish. I like that picture and I'm prepared –

HESTER (*angrily*). Please leave the subject. I wanted your opinion – not your money –

There is a knock on the door.

(*Calling.*) Who is that?

MILLER (*off*). Miller.

HESTER (*to* COLLYER). This is the man who looked after me this morning. I'd better let him in.

COLLYER *nods.* HESTER *opens the door.* MILLER *comes in, now dressed, but untidily.*

MILLER. I told you to stay in bed.

HESTER. Thanks to your ministrations, Mr. Miller, I feel perfectly all right now. This is Sir William Collyer – Mr. Miller.

The men nod to each other. MILLER *stares at* COLLYER *rather curiously.*

MILLER (*turning to* HESTER). Come down to the light. Just let me look. (*He examines her eyes.*) Tongue.

HESTER *extends her tongue.* MILLER *feels her pulse.*

Yes. You have a strong constitution. (*With a slight smile.*) You should live to a ripe old age.

HESTER (*matching his irony*). Barring accidents, of course.

He turns to go. COLLYER *stops him.*

COLLYER. Mr. Miller, I'm very grateful to you for all you did for my – for Mrs. Page –

MILLER. You needn't be, Sir William. I did very little for Mrs. Page.

COLLYER (*bristling a little*). I take it, Mr. Miller, that you're not a qualified medical practitioner?

MILLER. You take it quite correctly.

COLLYER. I only ask because a qualified doctor, in a case of this rather delicate kind, is strictly bound by a certain code.

MILLER. Yes, I've heard of it. It's much the same as the English schoolboy's code, isn't it? No sneaking.

COLLYER (*heavily*). I congratulate you on your knowledge of our idioms, Mr. Miller.

MILLER. I've spoken no other language since 1938, except for a year in the Isle of Man. Don't worry, Sir William. Or you – Mrs. Page. I won't sneak. I left a bottle of antiseptic in your bedroom. May I get it?

HESTER. Please.

He goes into the bedroom.

COLLYER. I don't think I like the look of him. I'm worried.

HESTER. He looks too much like a blackmailer to be one.

COLLYER. I don't share your confidence. Damn it! We ought at least to have offered him a fee –

HESTER. He wouldn't accept it. You'd insult him –

COLLYER. I wonder. It's a fair test.

MILLER *emerges from the bedroom with a bottle in his hand.*

Mr. Miller – if you were a qualified practitioner there is one other thing you would do.

MILLER *looks at* COLLYER *inquiringly.* COLLYER *takes out his wallet and pulls out a five-pound note, which he politely extends to* MILLER.

MILLER (*after a pause, with a faint smile*). Thank you. I'll send you a receipt.

He takes the note and goes out. COLLYER *makes an expressive gesture at* HESTER.

HESTER. You win.

COLLYER. The study of human nature is, after all, my profession. If there's any trouble from him, please get in touch with me at once.

HESTER (*wearily*). Yes, Bill.

COLLYER (*looking at his watch*). I must go. I have to be in court in fifteen minutes.

HESTER. Did you bring the car?

COLLYER. Yes.

HESTER. Still the Austin?

COLLYER. No. A new one. Or rather an older one – but a Rolls.

HESTER. Oh, I must have a look at it. (*She goes to the window and peers through. She darts back immediately.*) Oh Lord! You brought Flitton. I wonder who he thought you were going to visit in this low neighbourhood. You didn't tell him?

COLLYER. Of course not.

HESTER. How is he?

COLLYER. Very well.

HESTER. I miss him, you know. I miss them all. Even Miss Wilson. I bet she's been pounding that typewriter with a positive paean of triumph since I left.

COLLYER. There is, perhaps a certain added flourish to her style. (*He points to the picture over the fireplace.*) I do like that picture very much.

HESTER. You shall have it.

Pause.

COLLYER (*quietly*). Thank you very much. What a very handsome present!

HESTER *squeezes his hand gratefully.*

Which reminds me – many happy returns of yesterday.

HESTER. Thank you, Bill – (*Indicating the picture.*) Will you take this now, or shall I send it?

COLLYER (*after a slight pause*). May I call for it?

HESTER. When?

COLLYER. What time are you expecting Page?

HESTER. Not till about seven.

COLLYER. I'll come to tea.

HESTER. About five?

COLLYER. Five-twenty.

HESTER. Right!

COLLYER. Goodbye.

HESTER. Goodbye.

They shake hands, a little shyly.

COLLYER. I wish you'd try to find a way I could help you.

HESTER (*quietly*). I'll try to find a way.

> COLLYER *smiles back at her and goes.* HESTER, *left alone, takes a cigarette from her pocket. Then, having lit it, she goes to the window, concealing herself behind the curtains, but looking out. We hear the sound of a car door slam, and of the car drawing away.* HESTER *sighs. Then she goes to the sofa, lies down on it (her back to the door), and picks up a book. After a moment she puts the book down on her lap and stares sightlessly ahead. The door opens and* FREDDIE PAGE *comes in. He is in his late twenties or early thirties, with that sort of boyish good looks that does not indicate age. He carries a suitcase and a bag of golf clubs. The latter he deposits in a corner with a rattle. It is plain that* HESTER *has heard him come in, but she does not turn her head. During the ensuing scene she never looks at him at all, until the moment indicated later.*

FREDDIE. Hullo, Hes. How's tricks? I've just done ninety-three down the Great West. Alvis – smashing job. Jackie Jackson gave me a lift. We gave up the idea of playing golf. It started to rain. It's pouring down at Sunningdale. By the way, a bloody great Rolls was just moving off from here as I came in. I wonder whose it is, do you know?

> HESTER, *still staring ahead of her, does not reply.*

Do you think old Elton's lashed out and invested his life savings? Shouldn't be surprised, considering what he must make out of us.

HESTER. Did you have a good weekend?

FREDDIE. Not bad. Won both my matches. I took a fiver off Jackie. Match-bye and bye-bye. He was livid. I wanted to double the stakes – but he wouldn't wear it.

HESTER. How much did you win altogether?

FREDDIE. Seven.

HESTER. Can I have some of it – for Mrs. Elton?

FREDDIE. I thought you were going to sell those pictures. Is there any coffee left?

HESTER. I'm not now.

FREDDIE. Why not?

HESTER. I've given one away.

FREDDIE (*mildly*). That was a bloody silly thing to go and do, wasn't it?

HESTER. Yes. I suppose it was.

FREDDIE. Oh hell! All right. You can have three. I need the rest for lunch. I'm taking a South American to the Ritz. Get me giving lunch parties at the Ritz!

HESTER. What South American?

FREDDIE. Bloke I met at golf yesterday. Aircraft business. I got myself given the old intro to him – you know – one of England's most famous test pilots, D.F.C. and bar, D.S.O., all the old ex-Spitfire bull. He seemed impressed.

HESTER. So he should.

FREDDIE. Funny thing about gongs, when you think what a lottery they were. They don't mean a damn thing in war – except as a line-shoot, but in peacetime they're quite useful. This bloke's worth bags of dough. He's got some sort of tie-up with Vickers over here I think. He might fix something.

HESTER. I hope so.

FREDDIE. Anyway he ought to be good for a touch. I say – do you know you haven't looked at me once since I came in?

HESTER. Haven't I, Freddie?

FREDDIE. Why's that?

HESTER. I can remember what you look like.

FREDDIE *gets up from an armchair where he has been sprawling and goes over to* HESTER.

FREDDIE (*with a guilty look*). I haven't done anything, have I?

HESTER (*smiling*). No, Freddie. You haven't done anything.

FREDDIE. You're not peeved about last night, are you? You see, the blokes wanted to play again today, and if I'd let 'em down –

HESTER. That's all right.

FREDDIE. You were funny on the phone, too, I remember. There wasn't any special reason you wanted me back to dinner last night, was there?

HESTER, *still not looking at him, does not reply. She gets up from the sofa, her back to him. A sudden thought strikes* FREDDIE.

FREDDIE (*explosively*). Oh my God! (*After an embarrassed pause.*) Many happy returns!

HESTER. Thank you, Freddie.

FREDDIE. Blast! I remembered it on Saturday too. I was going past Barkers' and I thought, it's too late to get her a present now, I'll have to find a shop open on Sunday. Cigarettes, or something. Had you arranged anything special for dinner?

HESTER. Nothing very special. Steak and a bottle of claret.

FREDDIE. We'll have it tonight.

HESTER. Yes.

FREDDIE. Come on now, Hes. No more sulks, please. I've
said I'm sorry. I can't say more, can I?

HESTER. No. You can't say more.

FREDDIE (*coaxingly*). Come on, now. Give us a shot of those
gorgeous blue orbs. I haven't seen 'em for two whole days –

HESTER turns round and looks at him.

This is me. Freddie Page. Remember?

HESTER. I remember.

*He walks forward and kisses her. Instantly she responds,
with an intensity of emotion that is almost ugly. After a
moment he pushes her away and smacks her playfully.*

FREDDIE. Naughty to sulk with your Freddie. Go and get
dressed. We'll have a quick one at the Belvedere to
celebrate.

HESTER (*at the bedroom door*). Do you want me to lunch
with your South American?

FREDDIE. No. Better not. I can shoot a better line without
your beady eyes on me.

HESTER. They were gorgeous orbs a moment ago.

FREDDIE. They get beady in company. Go on, darling. Hurry.

HESTER (*who has been staring at him fixedly*). Yes.

FREDDIE (*jocularly*). Still love me?

HESTER (*steadily*). I still love you.

*She goes out. After a moment she opens the door again.
(Note – it opens inwards.) She is taking off her dressing-
gown as she speaks and hanging it up on a hook on the
door.*

Darling, where are you going to be between five and six?

FREDDIE. Nowhere particularly. Why?

HESTER. Do you mind being out? I've got someone coming
in I want to see alone.

FREDDIE. A customer?

HESTER. Yes.

FREDDIE. O.K. I'll go to that new club down the road.

HESTER (*smiling*). And don't get sozzled, either. Remember
our dinner.

FREDDIE. You shut up.

*She disappears, leaving the door open. We can hear bath
water being run.* FREDDIE *feels in his pocket for a
cigarette, and brings out an empty package.*

(*Calling.*) Darling – I'm out of cigarettes. Have you got
any?

HESTER (*off, calling*). There are some in my dressing-gown
pocket.

FREDDIE. Right.

He goes to the bedroom door and fumbles in the pocket of
HESTER*'s dressing-gown. He brings out a letter first, and
then the packet. He is about to replace the letter when he
glances at the envelope. He raises his eyebrows, and brings
the letter into the room. Sitting down, he lights a cigarette,
and then tears open the letter, and begins to read.*

HESTER (*off*). Have you got them?

FREDDIE (*his brows knit over the letter, which is a long one*).
What? Yes. I've got them, thanks. (*He continues to read.*)

Curtain.

ACT TWO

Scene: the same. It is now about five o'clock in the afternoon of the same day. FREDDIE *is sprawling, in the attitude in which we have already seen him, in one armchair, while his friend,* JACKIE JACKSON, *reclines in another. There is a bottle of whisky on the table, and a siphon, and both men are holding glasses.*

FREDDIE (*in an injured tone*). But it's too bloody silly, old boy – just because I forgot her birthday.

> JACKIE *makes a sympathetic sound.* FREDDIE *morosely takes another gulp of whisky.*

> My God – if all the men who forgot their wives' birthdays were to come home and find suicide notes waiting for them, the line of widowers would stretch from here to – to John o' Groats.

JACKIE. Further, old boy.

FREDDIE. You can't go further.

JACKIE. Well – from here to John o' Groats and back – and ending up at the Windmill, then.

FREDDIE (*angrily*). Shut up, Jackie. This isn't funny. I asked you round for help and advice and not to let loose a flood of corny wisecracks.

JACKIE. Sorry, Freddie, only the way you tell it, it sounds so idiotic. Are you sure it wasn't a joke, just to scare you?

FREDDIE. I've told you it wasn't.

> FREDDIE *has risen and is taking* JACKIE'*s glass from his willing hand for replenishment.*

JACKIE. Oh – thanks, old chap.

FREDDIE. I got the whole story out of old Ma Elton. She definitely tried to gas herself, and would have succeeded if there'd been a shilling in the blasted meter – (*He has replenished both glasses generously.*)

JACKIE. Well – that shows she couldn't have been too serious about it. (*Taking glass from* FREDDIE.) Oh, thanks. Cheers.

FREDDIE. Where's your imagination? If you're in a state of mind where you're going to try and bump yourself off, you don't think about things like meters.

JACKIE (*judiciously*). Well, I would.

FREDDIE. That from the man who once wrote off three Spits by forgetting to put his ruddy undercart down.

JACKIE. That was different. I wasn't trying to bump myself off.

FREDDIE. You gave a fairly good imitation of it –

JACKIE (*bridling*). At the Court of Inquiry it was definitely established –

FREDDIE. Oh shut up, Jackie. We're talking of something a good deal more important –

JACKIE. Well, you started it. All I said was – about the meter –

FREDDIE. I know what you said about the meter. But you're wrong. I've been into the whole thing, and you can take it from me that she did definitely try, last night, to kill herself.

JACKIE. And all because you forgot her birthday? But that's just the sort of black I'm always putting up with Liz.

FREDDIE. I know. I tell you, Jackie – it knocked me ruddy flat.

JACKIE. I can imagine.

FREDDIE (*explosively*). My God, aren't women the end!

JACKIE (*nodding sympathetically*). Where is she now?

FREDDIE. Out looking for me, I shouldn't wonder. (*He collects* JACKIE's *glass again.*)

JACKIE. No thanks.

FREDDIE *replenishes his own glass as he speaks.*

FREDDIE. She was having her bath. After I'd read that letter
I ran downstairs to Ma Elton and after that I just did a bunk.
I had to have a drink quick, and anyway I was damned if
I was going in to Hes and fall on my knees and say my
darling I have grievously sinned in forgetting your birthday;
if I promise you I'll never do it again, will you promise me
you'll never gas yourself again. I mean the whole thing's
too damn' idiotic –

JACKIE. There must be something else.

FREDDIE. There isn't anything else.

JACKIE (*tentatively*). Another girl?

FREDDIE. There never has been.

JACKIE. Had a lot of rows lately?

FREDDIE. No. As a matter of fact these last few months I've
been thinking we've been getting on better than before.

JACKIE (*evidently remembering Liz*). There must have been
some rows.

FREDDIE. Very minor ones. Nothing like the real flamers we
had when we first started.

JACKIE. What were they about?

FREDDIE (*uncomfortably*). Usual things.

JACKIE *waits for him to continue.*

(*Explosively.*) Damn it, Jackie, you know me. I can't be a
ruddy Romeo all the time.

JACKIE. Who can?

FREDDIE. According to her the whole damn' human race –
male part of it, anyway.

JACKIE. What does she know about it?

FREDDIE. Damn all. A clergyman's daughter, living in
Oxford, marries the first man who asks her and falls in love
with the first man who gives her an eye. (*After a slight
pause.*) Hell, it's not that I'm not in love with her too, of
course I am. Always have been and always will. But – well –

moderation in all things – that's always been my motto.
(*At the table.*) Have another?

JACKIE. Only a spot.

FREDDIE (*pouring himself one*). I've got nothing on my
conscience in that respect. I never gave myself that sort of
a build-up with her. She knew what she was taking on.

JACKIE. You don't think it's the marriage question that's upset
her?

FREDDIE. No. I'm the one that gets upset by that – not her.
Personally I can't wait for that divorce. All this hole-in-the-
corner stuff gets me down.

JACKIE. Doesn't it get her down too? I mean – a clergyman's
daughter?

FREDDIE. She jumped that fence a year ago. I was the one
that wanted to wait. She didn't. That was the first of our
flamers. (*He moodily sips his drink, lost in thought.*) My
God, it's so damned unfair. Supposing she'd pulled it off
last night, do you realize what everyone would have said?
That I'd bust up a happy marriage, and then driven Hes to
suicide. I'd have been looked on as a ruddy murderer. Did
she think of that, I wonder? Who the hell would have
believed what I've just told you?

JACKIE (*with unconscious irony*). Anyone who knows you.

FREDDIE. Yes, but this would have been front-page stuff.
All over the ruddy *News of the World,* Jackie. Think of that.
And this read out in court. (*He flourishes the letter.*) My
gosh, I'd have been lucky to have got out without being
lynched. The coroner would certainly have added a ruddy
rider. I was thinking at lunch today at the Ritz – I'd never
have been able to go into any restaurant again, without
people nudging and pointing –

JACKIE. Yes, I know. By the way, how did that go off – your
lunch with Lopez?

FREDDIE (*savagely*). Do you mind not changing the subject?
Or if I'm boring you with this story, just say so and we'll
have a little chat about the weather.

JACKIE. I'm sorry. I only wanted to know if he'd offered you anything. That's all. Go on about Hes, then.

FREDDIE (*muttering*). Hell. This is really getting me down. Sorry, Jackie. Didn't mean to bite your head off.

JACKIE. That's all right.

FREDDIE. Lopez? Yes, he offered me a job all right.

JACKIE. Good show.

FREDDIE (*sullenly*). Test pilot – in South America.

JACKIE. Oh Lord! I don't suppose you want to go to South America.

FREDDIE. I don't want to go anywhere – as a test pilot.

JACKIE. They say you were the tops.

FREDDIE. I was – a year ago. Since then things have changed a bit. (*He points to his glass.*) This stuff isn't exactly what the doctor ordered for nerve and judgment. Besides I'm too ruddy old. You're finished in that racket at twenty-five. I wouldn't last a week. I want something chairborne – not airborne. I've had flying for life. (*He rises to get another drink.*) Want one?

JACKIE. No, thanks. Do you think you ought to?

FREDDIE. I know I ought to. Why? Am I drunk?

JACKIE. No. It's only that I gather you've been at it most of the morning.

FREDDIE. And I shall be at it most of the evening too. I shall be at it until I've forgotten that this (*He indicates the letter.*) ever existed.

He gets himself a drink and slumps back into his chair. In speech and in manner he is not drunk, but from now on he is beginning to show some of the wildness and excitability of the habitual drinker who has had about his complement.

JACKIE (*pointing to the letter in* FREDDIE*'s hand*). Doesn't that give you any more clues?

FREDDIE. Read it and see.

JACKIE. No. I don't think so.

FREDDIE. Squeamish, aren't you?

JACKIE. Well – a thing like that – it's a bit – private, isn't it?

FREDDIE. Blasted private, it would have been, read out in court, by the coroner, wouldn't it?

JACKIE. There *is* that, I suppose.

FREDDIE. There *is* that, you suppose. All right. I'm the coroner. You're the public. Now listen. (*Reading.*) 'My darling – a moment ago, before I took the aspirin, I knew exactly what I wanted to say to you. I have run through this letter in my mind so very often and it has always been most eloquent and noble and composed. Now – those moving, pretty words just don't seem to be there. I think that's because, this time, I know I really am going to die.'

JACKIE (*acutely uncomfortable*). Look, old boy, don't go on. Knowing Hes as I do, I'd really rather not hear the rest –

FREDDIE. You're damn well going to hear the rest. I've got to read this to someone.

JACKIE. Still it's addressed to you and no one else.

FREDDIE. No one else – except, of course, the readers of all the Sunday papers. Listen, blast you. (*Reading.*) 'I know that, in the morning, when you read this letter, any feelings you ever had for me, and you had some, will be driven out of your heart for ever. Poor Freddie – poor darling Freddie. I'm so sorry.' (*To* JACKIE, *derisively.*) Sorry! All right. Here's your clue. (*Reading.*) 'You'll want to know why, and I'd so much like to make you understand, because if you understood you might forgive. But to understand what I'm doing now, you must feel even a small part of what I'm feeling now, and that I know you can never do. Just accept that it isn't your fault – it really isn't, Freddie – believe that. You can't help being as you are – I can't help being as I am. The fault lies with whichever of the gods had himself a good laugh up above by arranging for the two of us to meet –

HESTER *comes in quietly.* JACKIE *sees her and signals to* FREDDIE *who does not notice.*

Forgive my bad writing. I think perhaps the drug is beginning – '

HESTER (*in a cool voice*). Hullo, Jackie.

JACKIE. Hullo.

HESTER. How are you?

JACKIE. Very well, thanks, Hes.

HESTER. Where have you two been all afternoon?

JACKIE (*in an agony of embarrassment*). I haven't been with
Freddie. I was at home, and he rang up. Asked me over for
a chat –

HESTER. I see. (*To* FREDDIE.) Where were you, Freddie?

FREDDIE. A lot of places.

HESTER. I've been to most of them.

FREDDIE. I thought you might.

HESTER. Can I have that letter?

FREDDIE. Why?

HESTER. It belongs to me.

FREDDIE. There might be two views about that. It's got my
name on the envelope.

HESTER. An undelivered letter belongs, I should say, to the
sender. (*Lightly.*) Please.

HESTER *stands with her hand out, facing* FREDDIE. *He
gives her the letter and moves away from her. She tears
it up methodically and throws the pieces into the waste-
paper-basket. Then she takes the bottle of whisky and goes
over to a cupboard.*

FREDDIE. What are you doing?

HESTER. Tidying up.

FREDDIE. It's my bottle. I paid for it. (*He takes it away from
her and puts it back on the table.*)

HESTER (*lightly to* JACKIE). Did you have a good game yesterday, Jackie?

JACKIE. Yes, thanks.

HESTER. I hear Freddie beat you. He must be getting rather good.

JACKIE. Off that handicap, he is. It's a crying scandal. Look, Hes – I really think I ought to be dashing along.

HESTER. No, don't go, please. Freddie'll be going out in a minute or two, and I expect he'd like you to go with him. (*To* FREDDIE.) Darling, you hadn't forgotten about being out at five, had you?

FREDDIE. Yes. I had. What's the time now?

HESTER. Getting on. (*She goes to the picture she has given to her husband, and takes it down from the wall.*)

FREDDIE. And of course you don't want your respectable art lover to see me in my present state.

HESTER. I don't know anything about your present state, Freddie. I told you this morning I wanted you to be out.

FREDDIE (*pointing to the picture which she is now holding*). I thought you'd given that away.

HESTER. I have. I'm going to wrap it up.

FREDDIE. Then what are you going to sell this bloke?

HESTER (*at door, with a bright smile*). Whatever he wants to buy.

She goes out with the picture.

FREDDIE (*derisively at the closed door*). Ha! Ha!

JACKIE (*concerned*). Look, Freddie, old boy, I do think you ought to go and talk to her. I'll disappear –

FREDDIE. I've got time enough to talk to her. I've got a whole blasted lifetime to talk to her. You stay. (*He pours himself a drink.*)

JACKIE. Go easy on the Scotch, old boy.

FREDDIE. I've told you. I need it. Delicious oblivion.

JACKIE. Look, Freddie, old boy, I don't want to be rude, but you don't think perhaps, you might be dramatizing this thing a bit too much?

FREDDIE. Dramatizing? She's the one that's dramatizing. That cool, calm, collected act just now – you saw it. That's dramatizing – she enjoys that. I'm just a bloke who's having a couple of drinks because he's feeling ruddy miserable –

JACKIE. I don't expect she can be feeling exactly happy herself – whatever you say about her act just now.

FREDDIE. I suppose if she were Liz and you were in my place, you'd smother her with tender embraces –

JACKIE. I think I'd talk to her about it. I'd ask her what the trouble was, and what I could do to put it right –

FREDDIE. What the hell's the use of that? You heard that letter. Poor Freddie. You can't help being as you are. She's put her finger on it, all right. What am I supposed to do to put that little trouble right? Pretend to be something different? That'd be a lot of help, wouldn't it?

JACKIE. A few white lies –

FREDDIE. Don't be a clot. A few white lies! Dammit, man, talk sense. Do you think she's as easily fooled as that? You seem to see this as the sort of problem that that woman deals with in her advice column in the *Daily Whatsit* – a little domestic tiff that can be put right with a few kind words and a loving peck. Hes tried to kill herself last night.

JACKIE (*murmuring sadly*). I'm sorry, old boy. Perhaps I'm a bit out of my depth.

FREDDIE. Out of your depth? I should bloody well say you are. I'm out of my depth too, and it's a sensation I don't care for. My God, how I hate getting tangled up in other people's emotions. It's the one thing I've tried to avoid all my life, and yet it always seems to be happening to me. Always. (*After a pause.*) You remember Dot during the war, don't you? I brought her down to the squadron a couple of times?

JACKIE. Yes. I liked her a lot. A load of fun –

FREDDIE. A load of fun, until she started messing about with my service revolver.

JACKIE. She didn't –

FREDDIE. No. She didn't hurt herself or me or anyone else. Still you can imagine that the fun got a bit sour after that. And then there was – (*He stops.*) It doesn't matter. Too many emotions. Far too ruddy many. I loathe 'em.

JACKIE. A sort of *homme fatal,* eh?

FREDDIE (*quietly*). It's not so funny, you know, Jackie. It's not so funny. Hes says I've got no feelings and perhaps she's right, but anyway I've got something inside that can get hurt – the way it's hurt now. I don't enjoy causing other people misery. I'm not a ruddy sadist. My sort never gets a hearing. We're called a lot of rude names, and nobody ever thinks we have a case. But look at it this way, Jackie. Take two people – 'A' and 'B'. 'A' loves 'B' – 'B' doesn't love 'A', or at least not in the same way. He wants to, but he just can't. It's not his nature. Now 'B' hasn't asked to be loved. He may be a perfectly ordinary bloke, kind, well-meaning, good friend, perhaps even a good husband if he's allowed to be. But he's not allowed to be – that's my point. Demands are made on him which he just can't fulfil. If he tries, he's cheating, and cheating doesn't help anyone. Now if he's honest and doesn't try – well, then everyone says he's a skunk and a heartless cad, and coroners add ruddy riders. I mean – where are you? (*He finishes his drink.*) Come on. We'd better get weaving.

He goes to collect his coat. There is a knock on the door. FREDDIE *goes to open it.* MILLER *is outside.*

MILLER. Excuse me. Is Mrs. Page in?

FREDDIE. No, not at the moment. You're Mr. Miller, aren't you?

MILLER. Yes. And you are Mr. Page?

FREDDIE. That's right. Come in. I want to talk to you.

MILLER. Thank you.

FREDDIE. You looked after my wife, this morning, didn't you?

MILLER. Yes. I looked after Mrs. Page.

FREDDIE (*introducing*). This is Jackie Jackson. Mr. Miller.

The two men nod to each other.

(*To* MILLER.) Care for a drink?

MILLER. Thank you.

FREDDIE. I'd like to know how much she said to you. Mrs. Elton says you were with her alone. (*Indicating* JACKIE.) You needn't worry about him. He knows all about it.

MILLER. She said nothing.

FREDDIE. Nothing about why she did it?

MILLER. Nothing.

FREDDIE *hands him a drink.*

FREDDIE. Do you know why she did it?

MILLER. No.

FREDDIE. If you like I'll tell you.

JACKIE (*interposing*). No, Freddie –

FREDDIE. She did it because I forgot her birthday.

MILLER. Yes.

FREDDIE. You don't look surprised.

MILLER. I'm not. I assumed it was something of the kind.

FREDDIE. Something so trivial?

MILLER. Nothing can be called trivial that induces an operative desire to die.

FREDDIE. But forgetting a birthday –

MILLER. Yes. That is trivial.

FREDDIE. A riddler – this bloke. All right. What's the real reason, then? What's behind the triviality?

MILLER. I don't think you need me to tell you that.

FREDDIE. I'd like to hear it, anyway.

MILLER. Yourself, I should suppose.

FREDDIE. Which just about makes me a ruddy murderer.

MILLER (*politely*). A ruddy near-murderer.

JACKIE (*interposing*). Look – I don't think you ought to say a thing like –

FREDDIE. Shut up, Jackie. I can take it.

JACKIE. But he doesn't know the facts –

FREDDIE. The facts? What the hell do the facts matter? It's what's behind the facts that matters, isn't that so, Mr. Miller?

MILLER. Yes.

FREDDIE. And what's behind the facts is me.

MILLER. I imagine so.

FREDDIE. Little murdering me.

MILLER *nods.*

All right, my friend, and what would you do about it if you were me?

MILLER. That's a stupid question. Nature has not endowed me with the capacity for inspiring suicidal love.

FREDDIE. Aren't you lucky?

MILLER. Yes, I suppose I am.

FREDDIE. And what about a poor bloke who has this capacity for inspiring suicidal love – what does *he* do about it?

MILLER. Refuse to love at all, I'd say.

There is a pause. FREDDIE *turns to the bottle of whisky.*

FREDDIE. Have another drink. My God – we've had this bottle. (*He is pouring the last few drops into* MILLER*'s glass.*)

MILLER. Thank you.

FREDDIE. What you've just said, old boy, was a load of tripe.

MILLER. Very possibly. As this gentleman has already pointed out, I know nothing of the facts.

FREDDIE. One of the facts is that this character has no intention, at this stage in his life, of turning himself into a bloody hermit.

MILLER. No. I imagine he hasn't.

FREDDIE. You're damn' right, he hasn't, old boy. Look – let's continue this argument down the road. That new club opens at four.

JACKIE. Look, Freddie, I think I ought to be getting along. Liz'll be wondering –

FREDDIE (*ironically*). Liz'll be wondering. (*Waving at* JACKIE.) Portrait of a happily married man, Mr. Miller. A man who can be fairly certain of coming home and not finding his loving wife lying in front of a gas-fire –

HESTER *comes in, the picture now neatly wrapped and tied. She puts it away in a corner.*

HESTER (*to* MILLER). Oh hullo.

MILLER. Good afternoon.

JACKIE. I was just on my way, Hes.

HESTER. Must you go?

JACKIE. I must, I'm afraid. You're turning us out of the flat anyway, aren't you?

HESTER (*pleadingly*). Yes. But I hoped you'd keep Freddie company.

JACKIE. I'm afraid I can't, Hes. I've got people coming in.

FREDDIE. Bad luck, darling. No nurse for poor little Freddie-weddie –

He is putting on his coat, with slight difficulty. MILLER *helps him.*

Unless, of course, Mr. Miller here would like to volunteer for the job.

MILLER. I'm afraid I have some work to do.

FREDDIE. Work? What sort of work? Curing other people's love problems?

MILLER. No. Sending out a list of the latest prices for the St. Leger.

FREDDIE. You a bookie?

MILLER. Yes.

FREDDIE. I should never have thought it. What price is Makeshift?

MILLER. A hundred to seven.

FREDDIE. I'll have fifty to three-ten. That's to say if you'll accept me as a client –

MILLER *takes out a notebook and makes a note.*

MILLER. I'll submit your name to my proprietor.

FREDDIE. That's not you?

MILLER. Oh no. I'm only one of his many assistants.

JACKIE (*at the door*). Well, cheerio, Freddie. (*To* MILLER.) Goodbye.

HESTER. Give my love to Liz.

FREDDIE. You'd better not give her *my* love, Jackie. From all accounts it's pretty lethal.

JACKIE. Goodbye.

HESTER (*to* JACKIE). Goodbye.

JACKIE *goes.*

HESTER *waits at the door for* FREDDIE. *On his way there he stops at the table, picks up the bottle, and deposits it in the waste-paper basket.*

FREDDIE. Just tidying up. (*He walks on to the door.*)

HESTER (*trying to conceal her anxiety*). Freddie – I don't know that you should go out, you know.

FREDDIE. I thought you wanted me out. Your customer –

HESTER. Mrs. Elton can give him a message. He can come
back some other time. Why don't you go and have a good
lie down?

FREDDIE. No. I'm a good boy. When I'm told to go – I go –
(*He fumbles in his pockets. To* MILLER.) Can you lend me
a shilling?

MILLER *produces a shilling and gives it to him.* FREDDIE
throws it on to the table.

Just in case I'm late for dinner.

He goes out. HESTER *goes out on to the landing and
watches him go down the stairs. Though drunk his legs are
(and have been through the previous scene) supporting him
fairly steadily.* HESTER *turns back into the room.*

HESTER (*urgently*). Do you know where he's going?

MILLER. To the new club down the road.

HESTER. Are you really working, or was that just an excuse?

MILLER. I'm really working.

HESTER. Oh. (*She moves anxiously to the window.*)

MILLER. He'll be happier by himself than with me, you know.

HESTER. Why do you say that?

MILLER. Because I seem to have become the embodiment of
his conscience.

HESTER (*bitterly*). His conscience? You appear to have found
something in him that I've missed.

MILLER. They say the eyes of love are blind.

HESTER. They say that about the loved one's failings – not
about his virtues. And my eyes aren't blind. They can see,
quite well.

MILLER. I know they can. Too well.

HESTER *looks at him.*

To love with one's eyes open sometimes makes life very
difficult.

HESTER. Even – unbearable.

MILLER. I said – difficult.

HESTER. I don't like him being alone.

MILLER. Very well. I shall volunteer.

HESTER. Thank you very much, Mr. Miller. I'm very grateful.

MILLER. There's no need. (*Pointing to a picture.*) Did you paint that?

HESTER. Yes.

MILLER. I only ask because it doesn't seem to be at all in the style of the others.

HESTER. I was seventeen when I did that.

MILLER. Indeed. (*He examines it.*) Interesting. Did you go to Art School?

HESTER. No.

MILLER. There is a delicacy and freshness about this which is very striking.

HESTER. Hurry to Freddie, please. I'm very anxious.

There is a knock on the door. HESTER *goes to it and opens it.* COLLYER *is on the threshold. He comes in.*

You're early.

COLLYER. I know. I came straight from court.

MILLER. I'm just going, Sir William. I have an errand to perform for – Mrs. Page. Oh, by the way – I was going to put this in the post.

He takes an envelope from his pocket and hands it to COLLYER. *He goes out.*

HESTER. I ought to have asked you to phone me. Freddie came back unexpectedly and has only just gone out. (*Indicating envelope.*) What's that? Your receipt?

COLLYER. I imagine so. (*He opens the envelope and takes out a five-pound note.*) This is a piece of insolence. He's written on the back: 'For quasi-professional services, received with thanks. K. Miller.'

HESTER *smiles as* COLLYER *puts the note back in his case.*

Yes. I suppose the laugh is on me. What was this errand he was talking about?

HESTER. It doesn't matter. I promised you tea, didn't I?

COLLYER. Don't bother about tea. Moments are precious. I don't want you to waste them over a kettle in the kitchen. It's all right for me to stay for a moment or two, isn't it?

HESTER. Yes, Bill, I think so.

COLLYER. I saw Page just now.

HESTER. Did he see you?

COLLYER. No. I was in the car, just turning into this street. I put a newspaper up. He couldn't possibly have seen me. Besides he was quite obviously drunk.

HESTER. Oh? What makes you think that?

COLLYER. His passage down the street was rather erratic.

HESTER (*brightly*). I don't think it could have been Freddie you saw, Bill. He only left this flat a moment ago –

COLLYER (*reproachfully*). Hester – (*He indicates the glasses on the table.*)

HESTER. He'd been having a drink with a friend.

COLLYER *picks out of the waste-paper basket the empty bottle, the head of which is showing.*

HESTER (*angrily*). Really, Bill. Even a judge can let his imagination run away with him. (*She takes the bottle and puts it away in a cupboard.*)

COLLYER. How long has it been going on?

HESTER. How long has what been going on?

COLLYER. In the old days he hardly touched alcohol.

HESTER (*shortly*). Is that so? I don't remember.

COLLYER. Of course you remember. He never drank at Sunningdale. He used to say it was bad for his judgment as a pilot.

HESTER (*quietly*). Very well, then, Bill. If in the last ten months Freddie's taken to drink, it must be I who've driven him to it.

COLLYER (*equally quietly*). And he who's driven you to suicide.

HESTER. No. I drove myself there.

Pause.

COLLYER. Hester, what's happened to you?

HESTER. Love, Bill, that's all – you know – that thing you read about in your beloved Jane Austen and Anthony Trollope. Love. 'It droppeth as the gentle dew from heaven.' No. That's wrong, isn't it? I know. 'It comforteth like sunshine after rain – '

COLLYER. Rather an unfortunate quotation. Go on with it.

HESTER. I can't. I've forgotten.

COLLYER. 'Love comforteth like sunshine after rain and Lust's effect is tempest after sun.'

HESTER. Tempest after sun? That would be very apt, wouldn't it, if that were all I felt for Freddie.

COLLYER. In sober truth, Hester, isn't it?

HESTER (*angrily*). Oh, God, Bill, do you really think I can tell you the sober truth about what I feel for Freddie? I've got quite a clear mind – too clear, I've just been told – and if it were only my *mind* that were involved . . . But in sober truth, Bill – in sober truth neither you nor I nor anyone else can explain what I feel for Freddie. It's all far too big and confusing to be tied up in such a neat little parcel and labelled lust. Lust isn't the whole of life – and Freddie is, you see, to me. The whole of life – and of death, too, it seems. Put a label on that, if you can – (*She turns abruptly.*) Gosh! I wish Freddie hadn't drunk all the whisky.

COLLYER. Would you like to go out?

HESTER. No. I'd better stay in and await developments.

COLLYER. What developments?

HESTER. Oh – quite a large variety are apt to offer themselves when Freddie's on the rampage –

She sits down, facing away from COLLYER. *There is a pause while he stares at her.*

COLLYER (*at length*). What made us choose Sunningdale that summer?

HESTER (*at the window*). It was your idea. You wanted the golf.

COLLYER. You weren't keen, I remember. You'd have preferred the sea.

HESTER (*absently*). Yes.

Pause.

COLLYER. You know you never told me exactly how it first happened.

HESTER. No. I suppose I didn't.

There is a pause before she begins. While she speaks she does not look at COLLYER. *It is almost as though she were talking to herself.*

It was the day you were playing for the President's Cup.

COLLYER. Oh yes, I remember.

HESTER. I came up to the golf club to collect you to go on to that party at the Hendersons'. You were still out playing. Freddie was there alone. He'd been chucked for a game and was bad-tempered. I'd met him several times before up at the club with the others – but I'd never paid much attention to him. I didn't think he was even particularly good-looking, and the R.A.F. slang used to irritate me slightly I remember. It's such an anachronism now, isn't it – as dated as gad-zooks and odds my life.

COLLYER. He does it for effect, I suppose.

HESTER. No. He does it because his life stopped in 1940. He loved 1940, you know. There were some like that. He's never been really happy since he left the R.A.F. (*After a slight pause.*) Well – that day you were a long time over your game.

COLLYER. Yes. We were held up badly, I remember.

HESTER. And Freddie and I sat on the veranda together for at least an hour. For some reason he talked very honestly and rather touchingly about himself – how worried he was about his future, how his life seemed to have no direction or purpose, how he envied you – the brilliant lawyer –

COLLYER. That was good of him.

HESTER. He meant it sincerely. Then quite suddenly he put his hand on my arm and murmured something very conventional, about envying you for other reasons besides your career. I laughed at him and he laughed back, like a guilty small boy. He said, 'I really do, you know, it's not just a line. I really think you're the most attractive girl I've ever met.' Something like that. I didn't really listen to the words, because anyway I knew then in that tiny moment when we were laughing together so close that I had no hope. No hope at all.

Pause.

COLLYER. It was that night that you insisted on coming up to London with me, wasn't it?

HESTER. Yes.

COLLYER. You didn't want to come back to Sunningdale the next weekend either, I remember –

HESTER. No.

COLLYER. When, exactly –

HESTER. It was in September. Do you remember I went up to London with him to see a play?

COLLYER. But that meeting in the clubhouse was in June.

HESTER. June the twenty-fourth.

COLLYER (*quietly*). During those two months, why didn't you talk to me about it?

HESTER. What would you have said to me if I had?

COLLYER. What I say now. That this man you say you love is morally and intellectually a mile your inferior and has absolutely nothing in common with you whatever; that what you're suffering from is no more than an ordinary and rather sordid infatuation; and that it's your plain and simple duty to exert every effort of will you're capable of in order to return to sanity at once.

HESTER *nods quietly. There is a pause.*

And how would you have answered that?

HESTER. By agreeing with you, I suppose. But it wouldn't have made any difference. (*She looks at her watch.*)

COLLYER (*at length*). If we'd been able to have a child, how much difference would it have made?

HESTER (*after a pause*). Isn't reality enough to occupy us, Bill?

COLLYER. Meaning, I suppose, that it would have made no difference at all?

HESTER. That's not what I said.

COLLYER. It's fantastic to think what was caused by my decision to rent that damn villa.

HESTER. Don't distress yourself with that sort of thought, Bill. Freddie and I would have met anyway. I think it's time you went.

COLLYER (*ironically*). You believe in affinities?

HESTER (*simply*). I believe it was fated that Freddie and I should meet.

COLLYER. As it's turned out, a pretty evil fate.

HESTER. If there are good affinities there must be evil ones too, I suppose. Don't forget your present, after all the trouble I've been to wrapping it up.

She goes to the parcel and picks it up. A key is suddenly turned in the door and it is thrown open, revealing FREDDIE. He stands for a time in the doorway, looking from COLLYER to HESTER. Then he comes in and closes the door behind him. He appears to have sobered up a little.

FREDDIE. I thought it might be. Not many people who come to this place have a big black Rolls.

HESTER. Where's Miller?

FREDDIE. Miller?

HESTER. Didn't you see him at the club?

FREDDIE. I never went to the club. (*To* COLLYER.) That's the same chauffeur, isn't it?

COLLYER. Yes.

HESTER. Bill came to see me because someone telephoned to him about my accident.

FREDDIE. Yes. (*To* COLLYER.) You've heard about her – accident, have you?

COLLYER. Yes.

FREDDIE. Did you ever forget her birthday?

COLLYER. No.

FREDDIE. No. I shouldn't think you were a forgetful type. You're a judge now, aren't you?

COLLYER. Yes.

FREDDIE. Still making packets of money?

COLLYER. A certain amount.

FREDDIE. Still love Hes?

HESTER (*sharply*). Don't listen to him, Bill. He's drunk. Freddie, you'd better go and lie down.

FREDDIE. See how I'm bullied? I bet you were never bullied like that.

HESTER. Freddie, please try and behave yourself.

FREDDIE. Am I behaving badly? I'm only asking the judge here a simple question. I'd rather like to know the answer. Still, I suppose it doesn't really matter –

He goes into the bedroom, and we hear the door bolted.

HESTER. I'm sorry, Bill.

COLLYER. That's all right.

HESTER. I think perhaps you'd better go.

COLLYER. Yes.

He moves towards his hat and coat, picks them up, and then hesitates uncertainly. HESTER is not looking at him, but at the bedroom door.

The answer to that question is yes, you know.

HESTER (*not having understood*). What?

COLLYER. The question Page asked me just now. The answer is yes.

Pause.

HESTER. Bill – please don't –

COLLYER. I'm sorry. (*Indicating bedroom.*) Sure you can cope with the – situation?

HESTER. Oh heavens, yes. This is nothing.

COLLYER. He's changed a lot. He looks quite different.

HESTER. He hasn't been well lately.

COLLYER. No. (*He stretches out his hand.*) Well, goodbye.

HESTER. I'm sorry, Bill. I'm so sorry. Is there anything more I can say?

COLLYER. I don't think so.

He smiles at her. HESTER kisses him suddenly on the cheek.

HESTER. Goodbye, Bill.

COLLYER *smiles at her again and goes.* HESTER *closes the door behind him and then goes quickly to the bedroom door. She knocks.*

HESTER (*calling*). Freddie, let me in, darling.

There is no answer. She knocks again.

Freddie – don't be childish. Let me in.

There is no answer. HESTER *walks away from the door and goes to get a cigarette. As she is lighting it* FREDDIE *emerges from the bedroom. He has changed into a blue suit.*

Why, Freddie, you're looking very smart. Going out somewhere?

FREDDIE. Yes.

HESTER. Where?

FREDDIE. To see a man about a job.

HESTER. What man?

FREDDIE. Lopez. I've just called him.

HESTER. Lopez?

FREDDIE. The South American I had lunch with.

HESTER. Oh yes, of course. I'd forgotten. How did it go off?

FREDDIE. It went off all right.

HESTER. Oh good. You think you'll get the job?

FREDDIE. Yes, I think so. He made a fairly definite offer. Of course it's up to his boss.

HESTER. Let's have a look at you. (*She inspects him.*) Oh, darling, you might have changed your shirt.

FREDDIE. Well, I hadn't a clean one.

HESTER. No. Nor you had. The laundry's late again this week. I'll wash one out for you tomorrow.

FREDDIE. Yes. Does it look too bad?

HESTER. No. It'll pass. Your shoes need a clean.

FREDDIE. Yes. I'll give them a rub.

HESTER. No. Take them off. I'll do them. (*She goes towards the kitchen.*) Somehow or other you always manage to get shoe polish over your face – Lord knows how.

She disappears into the kitchen. FREDDIE *takes his shoes off.* HESTER *comes back with shoe brushes and a tin of polish. She takes the shoes from him and begins to clean them. There is a fairly long silence.*

What's the job?

FREDDIE (*muttering*). Yes. I suppose I must tell you.

HESTER *gives him a quick glance.*

HESTER. Yes, Freddie. I think I'd like to know.

FREDDIE. Look, Hes. I've got to talk for a bit now. It's not going to be easy, so don't interrupt, do you mind? You always could argue the hind leg off a donkey – and just when I've got things clear in my mind I don't want them muddled up again.

HESTER. I'm sorry, Freddie. I must interrupt at once. The way you've been behaving this afternoon, how could you have things clear in your mind?

FREDDIE. I'm all right now, Hes. I had a cup of black coffee and after that a bit of a walk. I know what I'm doing.

HESTER. And what are you doing, Freddie?

FREDDIE. Accepting a job in South America as a test pilot.

HESTER. Test pilot? But you've said a hundred times you could never go back to that. After that crash in Canada you told me you had no nerve or judgment left.

FREDDIE. They'll come back. I had too many drinks that time in Canada. You know that.

HESTER. Yes, I know that. So did the Court of Inquiry know that. Does this man Lopez know that?

FREDDIE. No, of course not. He won't hear either. Don't worry about my nerve and judgment, Hes. A month or two

on the wagon and I'll be the old ace again – the old dicer
with death.

HESTER (*sharply*). Don't use that idiotic R.A.F. slang, Freddie.
(*More gently.*) Do you mind? This is too important –

FREDDIE. Yes. It is important.

HESTER. Whereabouts in South America?

FREDDIE. Somewhere near Rio.

HESTER. I see. (*She continues to clean the shoes mechanically.*) Well, when do we start?

FREDDIE. We don't.

HESTER. We don't?

FREDDIE. You and I don't. That's what I'm trying to tell you.
I'm going alone.

HESTER *lays the shoe down quietly, staring at* FREDDIE.

HESTER (*at length*) Why, Freddie?

FREDDIE. If I'm to stay on the wagon, I've got to be alone.

HESTER (*in a near whisper*). Have you?

FREDDIE. Oh hell – that's not the real reason. Listen, Hes,
darling.

*There is a pause while he paces the room as if concen-
trating desperately on finding the words.* HESTER *watches
him.*

You've always said, haven't you, that I don't really love
you? Well, I suppose, in your sense I don't. But what I do
feel for you is a good deal stronger than I've ever felt for
anybody else in my life, or ever will feel, I should think.
That's why I went away with you in the first place, that's
why I've stayed with you all this time, and that's why I
must go away from you now.

HESTER (*at length*). That sounds rather like a prepared
speech, Freddie.

FREDDIE. Yes. I suppose it is. I worked it out on my walk.
But it's still true, Hes. I'm too fond of you to let things

slide. That letter was a hell of a shock. I knew often you
were unhappy – you often knew I was a bit down too. But
I hadn't a clue how much the – difference in our feelings
had been hurting you. It's asking too damn' much of any
bloke to go on as if nothing had happened when he knows
now for a fact that he's driving the only girl he's ever loved
to suicide.

HESTER (*in a low voice*). Do you think your leaving me will
drive me away from suicide?

FREDDIE (*simply*). That's a risk I shall just have to take, isn't
it? It's a risk both of us will have to face.

Pause.

HESTER. Freddie – you mustn't scare me like this.

FREDDIE. No scare, Hes. Sorry, this is on the level.

HESTER. You know perfectly well you'll feel quite differently
in the morning.

FREDDIE. No, I won't, Hes. Not this time. Besides I don't
think I'll be here in the morning.

HESTER. Where will you be?

FREDDIE. I don't know. Somewhere. I think I'd better get out
tonight.

HESTER. No, Freddie. No.

FREDDIE. It's better that way. I'm scared of your arguing.
(*Passionately*). I know this is right, you see. I know it, but
with your gift of the gab, you'll muddle things up for me
again, and I'll be lost.

HESTER. I won't Freddie. I won't. I promise I won't. But you
must stay tonight. just tonight.

FREDDIE (*unhappily*). No, Hes.

HESTER. Just tonight, Freddie. Only one night.

FREDDIE. No. Sorry, Hes.

HESTER. Don't be so cruel, Freddie. How can you be so
cruel?

FREDDIE. Hes – this is our last chance. If we miss it, we're done for. We're death to each other, you and I.

HESTER. That isn't true.

FREDDIE. It is true, darling, and you've known it longer than I have. I'm such a damn' fool and that's been the trouble, or I should have done this long ago. That's it, you know. It's written in great bloody letters of fire over our heads – 'You and I are death to each other.'

HESTER *is unrestrainedly weeping.* FREDDIE *comes over to her and picks up his shoes.*

HESTER. I haven't finished them.

FREDDIE. They're all right. (*He begins to put them on.*) I'm sorry, Hes. Oh God, I'm sorry. Please don't cry. You don't know what it does to me.

HESTER. Not now. Not this minute. Not this minute, Freddie?

FREDDIE *finishes putting on his shoes, and then turns away from her, brushing his sleeve across his eyes.*

HESTER (*going to him*). You've got all your things here. You've got to pack –

FREDDIE. I'll send for them.

HESTER. You promised to come back for dinner.

FREDDIE. I know. I'm sorry about that. (*He kisses her quickly and goes to the door.*)

HESTER (*frantically*). But you can't break a promise like that, Freddie. You can't. Come back just for our dinner, Freddie. I won't argue, I swear, and then if you want to go away afterwards –

FREDDIE *goes out.* HESTER *runs to the door after him.*

Freddie, come back. . . . Don't go. . . . Don't leave me alone tonight . . . Not tonight . . . Don't leave me alone tonight . . .

She has followed him out as the curtain falls.

ACT THREE

Scene: the same.

At the rise of the curtain HESTER *is sitting, motionless and tense, staring unblinkingly at some object straight ahead of her. After an appreciable pause the telephone rings.* HESTER's *reaction is indicative of the nervous tension which she is undergoing. She reaches for the receiver, then drops her hand, and, standing close to the telephone, allows it to ring for a few times before she takes the receiver off.*

HESTER. Hullo? . . . Oh. No, he's not in, I'm afraid . . . Yes, it is. Who is that? . . . Oh. Yes. Good evening . . . I don't know exactly when he'll be back. What's the time now? . . . Eleven ten? Is it as late as that? . . . Oh no. I wasn't asleep – just reading. . . . Yes, I expect him in quite soon. . . . It's about golf? Yes, I'll get him to ring you. He knows your number, doesn't he? . . . Quite all right. Good night.

She replaces the receiver and now stands for a little time staring at it. After a moment impulsively she puts her hand out to take the receiver, stops – with her hand still out-stretched – then drops it hopelessly. She turns away from it, and walks back to her chair, resuming exactly the same pose in which we first discovered her. There is a knock on the door. HESTER *opens it.* MRS. ELTON *is outside.*

MRS. ELTON. Hullo, dear.

HESTER. Yes, Mrs. Elton?

MRS. ELTON. Just thought I'd pop up and see how you were. (*Looking round.*) Mr. Page not in?

HESTER. No.

MRS. ELTON. Don't you want the fire on? It's turned quite cold all of a sudden.

HESTER. No, thank you.

MRS. ELTON. Fancy not drawing the curtains.

There is a knock on the half-opened door and ANN WELCH *puts a tentative head round the door.*

ANN. Oh. Excuse me.

HESTER. Good evening.

ANN. Good evening, Mrs. Page. I just wondered if Philip was here, by any chance –

HESTER. Philip? Oh, your husband. No. Why should he be?

ANN. I thought perhaps Mr. Page was back and –

HESTER (*excitedly*). Is he with him?

ANN. Yes, I think so.

HESTER. Where?

ANN. Well, I don't know. I didn't want to go with them because I had some work to do. Still, they've been gone nearly two hours now and –

HESTER (*to* ANN). How did you meet him?

ANN. We were having our dinner at the Belvedere – and Mr. Page was in the bar and then he came up and sat at our table.

HESTER. I see.

ANN. Of course we hardly know him at all, you know, but he was very nice and friendly and said he wanted company, and he gave us a brandy each, and then, after that, he asked Philip to go on with him to this new club for a few moments.

HESTER. Which new club?

ANN. I'm afraid I can't remember the name.

HESTER. How was he?

ANN. Do you mean was he – ?

HESTER. Drunk, yes.

ANN. Well, I wouldn't actually say drunk. Of course that was two hours ago. Philip doesn't drink at all, of course, so that's all right. The only thing is . . . I know it's awfully silly of me . . . but I'm not very good at being left alone.

HESTER (*with a faint smile*). Yes, Mrs. Welch. I understand. Well, you mustn't worry. I expect your husband will be back very soon.

ANN. Oh yes. I expect so. If he comes in here, send him straight up, won't you?

HESTER. I will. Good night.

ANN. Good night.

She goes.

HESTER. Mrs. Elton, do you remember the name of the new club?

MRS. ELTON. No, dear. I don't, I'm afraid.

HESTER. I remember a card came – (*Suddenly.*) The Crow's Nest!

She goes quickly to the telephone book, and begins to search.

MRS. ELTON. That's right. I knew it was something like that.

She watches HESTER *sympathetically as she finds the number and begins to dial.*

HESTER. Hullo? . . . Oh, tell me, is Mr. Page there? . . . Mr. Page . . . Yes, that's right . . . Yes. Oh. How long ago? . . . Half an hour. I see. Do you know where he went? No. It doesn't matter . . . If he comes in again tell him his wife called – (*Frantically.*) no, hold on – waiter – don't tell him anything – anything at all . . . Yes, that's right. Good night.

She rings off. MRS. ELTON *shakes her head.*

MRS. ELTON. I can't understand how he could go and do a thing like that – leaving you alone tonight after what happened –

HESTER (*abruptly*). Mrs. Elton – haven't you got work to do?

MRS. ELTON (*quietly*). Yes, dear. Plenty. (*She goes to the door.*)

HESTER (*quickly*). I'm sorry. I didn't mean to be unkind.

MRS. ELTON (*turning*). Oh, you don't need to tell me. You couldn't mean to be unkind. You're not that sort. I'll let you into a little secret. You're my favourite tenant.

HESTER. Am I?

MRS. ELTON (*nodding*). Sad, isn't it, how one always seems to prefer nice people to good people, don't you think?

She has opened the door. MILLER, *wearing an overcoat, is outside. He is carrying a rather large leather bag.*

Oh, good evening, Mr. Miller. You're back from your work early.

MILLER. Yes. (*To* HESTER.) How are you tonight, Mrs. Page?

HESTER. Quite well, thank you. Do you usually work as late as this?

MILLER. Sometimes.

HESTER. What have you got in that formidable looking bag?

MILLER. It is nothing. Nothing at all. (*He turns to go on up the stairs.*)

MRS. ELTON. Oh, Mr. Miller, I don't like to ask you but I wonder if you'd just have a look at Mr. Elton tonight. He's bad again.

MILLER. I'll come down in five minutes.

MRS. ELTON. Thank you ever so much. I'm very grateful.

He goes on up the stairs.

You shouldn't have asked him that about the bag, dear. He hates to tell.

HESTER (*abstractedly*). I'm sorry. I wasn't really curious. Just talking for the sake of talking. (*She is staring at the telephone.*)

MRS. ELTON. If I were you, dear, I wouldn't use that thing again tonight.

HESTER. Perhaps you're right. (*She sits down.*)

MRS. ELTON. Why not go to bed? I'll bring you a nice warm drink –

HESTER *shakes her head.*

Or I'll get Dr. Miller to give you one of his sleeping pills –

HESTER. He *is* a doctor, of course, isn't he?

MRS. ELTON. Well. He was.

HESTER. I see. I knew he'd been in trouble.

MRS. ELTON. How, dear?

HESTER. Fellow-feeling, I suppose.

MRS. ELTON. Yes, he *was* in trouble once. Bad trouble.

HESTER *nods.*

Don't say I told you, will you? Poor Mr. Miller! I'm sorry for him. So ashamed of people knowing –

HESTER. Did he tell you about it?

MRS. ELTON. No, dear. Just after he'd come here there was a letter for him addressed to 'Kurt Miller, M.D.' – and then of course I remembered the case, because there'd been quite a lot in the papers about it. Of course I didn't let on to him I knew, but he guessed I did all right, because one day when I was saying how tidy he always kept his room, 'Well,' he said, 'Mrs. Elton, I suppose tidiness is the only lesson I ever did learn in jail.' Just like that. That was the only time he ever mentioned it, but it was quite soon after that he volunteered to look after Mr. Elton. I think it's a wicked shame the way they've treated him. Imagine a man like that being a bookmaker's clerk. There's waste for you, if you like.

HESTER. Why did he take the job?

MRS. ELTON. Because beggars can't be choosers, dear, and if a patient of his that was a bookie takes pity on him – well, he's got to eat, hasn't he? Anyway I can tell you what's in that bag if you really want to know. He goes and works every night in a hospital for infantile paralysis – unpaid, of course. That was his speciality before – apparently he was working on some sort of treatment –

HESTER. Won't he ever get back on the Medical Register?

MRS. ELTON. Oh no. Not a hope, I should say, dear. You know what they're like, and what he did wasn't – well – the sort of thing people forgive very easily. Ordinary normal people, I mean.

HESTER. You've forgiven it, Mrs. Elton.

MRS. ELTON. Oh well, I see far too much of life in this place to get upset by that sort of thing. It takes all sorts to make a world, after all – doesn't it? There was a couple once in Number Eleven – (*She stops suddenly.*) I can hear him on the stairs.

She opens the door. MILLER *is descending the stairs.*

I'll go down and get Mr. Elton ready, shall I?

MILLER. Yes.

MRS. ELTON. I wonder if you'd be kind enough to give Mrs. Page one of your sleeping pills.

MILLER. I'd thought of that myself.

MRS. ELTON. Good. (*To* HESTER.) Well, good night, dear. If you want anything just give me a ring. I'll be up with Mr. Elton most of the night anyway.

She goes. MILLER *comes into the room, takes a bottle from his pocket, and shakes out two pills which he hands to* HESTER.

HESTER. Thank you, Doctor. (*She puts them down on the table.*)

MILLER. I've asked you before not to call me that.

HESTER. I keep forgetting. I'm sorry.

MILLER. Are you going to bed now?

HESTER. In a moment.

MILLER (*turning to go*). Don't let that moment be too long.

HESTER. Everyone is very solicitous of me this evening.

MILLER. Are you surprised? Voices carry on the stairs of this house.

HESTER. Freddie's and mine?

MILLER *nods.*

Everyone heard us, I suppose. All the respectable tenants nudging each other and saying there's that woman's drunken boy friend walking out on her. Serve her right.

MILLER. I didn't say that. But then, of course, I may not be a respectable tenant.

HESTER (*simply*). What should I do?

MILLER. What makes you think I can tell you?

HESTER. How near did *you* come to the gas-fire, once?

Pause. MILLER *turns abruptly away from her.*

MILLER. Mrs. Elton, eh? (*He turns back to face her. Abruptly.*) You ask my advice. Take those pills and sleep tonight. In the morning – go on living.

There is a knock on the door. HESTER *opens it.* COLLYER *is outside, dressed in a dinner jacket.*

HESTER. Bill –

COLLYER. I don't apologize. I've got to see you –

He comes in, glancing at MILLER *as he does so.*

MILLER (*to* HESTER). Yes. That is the most specific advice I can give you. Good night.

He nods to COLLYER *and goes out.* COLLYER *silently hands her an opened letter which he has been holding in his hand.* HESTER *draws in her breath sharply as she sees the handwriting. She reads it through quickly.*

HESTER. When did it arrive?

COLLYER. I don't know. It was found about twenty minutes ago. I gather he dropped it in the box without ringing the bell.

HESTER *re-reads the letter, absently.*

It *is* true, I suppose?

HESTER (*wearily*). Yes. It's true. (*She hands the letter back.*)

COLLYER. When?

HESTER. This afternoon. Just after you'd left.

COLLYER. What was the reason?

HESTER. What happened last night. That's why he was drunk this afternoon. He said we were death to each other –

COLLYER. *In vino veritas.*

HESTER. He wasn't so drunk when he said that.

COLLYER. Then he has more perception than I gave him credit for. What's he going to do?

HESTER. He's taken a job as a test pilot in South America.

COLLYER. I see. (*Glancing at the letter.*) I rather like the phrase: 'Sorry to have caused so much bother.' It has a nice ring of R.A.F. understatement –

He tears the letter up and throws it into the waste-paper basket.

(*After a pause.*) I'm awfully sorry for you, Hester.

HESTER (*her back to him*). That's all right. It was bound to happen one day, I suppose.

COLLYER. I have a faint inkling of how you must be feeling at this moment.

HESTER (*turning. Hard and bright*). Oh, I'll get over it I imagine. You're looking very smart. Where have you been?

COLLYER. At home. I had some people in to dinner.

HESTER. Who?

COLLYER. Olive, the Prestons, an American judge and his
wife –

HESTER. Was Olive in good form?

COLLYER. Fairly. She said one very funny thing.

HESTER. What was it?

COLLYER. Damn. I've forgotten. Oh yes. I do remember.
Now I come to think of it, it's not all that funny. It must
have been the way she said it. She told the American judge
he had a face like an angry cupid –

HESTER. An angry cupid? I can just hear her –

*She starts to laugh, and then continues longer than the joke
appears to warrant.*

An angry cupid!

*The laugh suddenly turns into sobs. She buries her head in
the sofa cushion, desperately but unsuccessfully trying to
control her emotion.* COLLYER *sits beside her.*

COLLYER. Hester. please. If only I could say something that
would help you. (*He strokes her head.*)

HESTER *is succeeding now in recovering herself.*

I know it's small comfort to you at this moment, but this
must be for the best. You yourself spoke of an evil affinity,
didn't you?

HESTER, *wiping her eyes, does not reply.* COLLYER *looks
round the room.*

HESTER. I'm sorry about that. I couldn't help it –

COLLYER. You must get out of this flat as soon as possible.
In fact I don't think you should be left alone in it at all.

HESTER. I'll be all right.

COLLYER. I'm not so sure. I think you'd better leave here
tonight.

HESTER. Tonight?

COLLYER. You were alone here last night, weren't you?

HESTER. Where could I go?

COLLYER. Well – I could make a very tentative suggestion. In fact the suggestion that Freddie makes in that letter.

HESTER. No, Bill. That's impossible.

COLLYER. Have you forgotten so quickly what I told you this afternoon?

HESTER (*her voice rising*). Stop it, Bill – please –

He is silenced by the note of strain in her voice. She gets up, a little unsteadily, and goes to a cupboard.

I expect you'd like a drink, wouldn't you?

COLLYER. A good idea.

HESTER. Oh dear! I'd forgotten that Freddie had finished the whisky.

COLLYER. It doesn't matter.

HESTER. Wait a moment. Here's something. (*She brings out a bottle of wine.*) Claret. I'm afraid I uncorked it last night. It's from the local grocer. I don't know what your fastidious palate will make of it.

COLLYER. I'm sure it's delicious. (*He opens the bottle.*)

She gives him two glasses. He fills them.

Well? What shall the toast be?

HESTER. The future, I suppose.

COLLYER. May I say our future?

HESTER (*gravely*). No, Bill. Just the future.

They drink in silence.

Is it all right?

COLLYER. Very good. (*After another pause.*) And what's the future to be?

HESTER. I haven't thought yet.

COLLYER. Don't you think you should?

HESTER. I'll stay on here until I can find somewhere else.
I'll try and take a studio if I can – then I'll be able to work
harder. If I can't sell my paintings, I'll get a job –

COLLYER. What sort of job?

HESTER. There must be something I can do.

COLLYER (*quietly*). And you contemplate living alone for the
rest of your life?

HESTER. I don't contemplate anything, Bill. I'm not exactly
in a contemplative mood.

COLLYER. When you are, I'd like you to contemplate a very
different future –

HESTER (*angrily*). Bill, please, I've asked you –

COLLYER (*equally angrily*). Hester, for God's sake, don't you
realize what I'm offering you?

HESTER. And don't *you* realize how difficult it is for me to
refuse?

COLLYER. Then why need you refuse?

HESTER. Because I must. I can't go back to you as your wife,
Bill, because I no longer am your wife. We can't wipe out
this last year as if it had never happened. Don't you understand that?

COLLYER. I only understand that I'm even more in love with
you now than I was on our wedding day.

HESTER (*quietly*). You weren't in love with me on our
wedding day, Bill. You aren't in love with me now, and you
never have been.

COLLYER. Hester!

HESTER. I'm simply a prized possession that has now become
more prized for having been stolen, that's all.

COLLYER (*hurt*). What are you saying?

HESTER (*upset*). You force me to say these things, Bill. Do you think I enjoy hurting you, of all people? Perhaps you'd better go now, and we can talk some other time, when we both feel calmer.

COLLYER. We must talk now. You say I wasn't in love with you when I married you?

HESTER. I know you weren't.

COLLYER. Then why do you suppose I married you? What else did you have to offer me?

HESTER (*interrupting*). I know, Bill, I know. You don't need to remind me of what a bad match I was. I was always very conscious of it. Oh, I'm not denying you married for love – for your idea of love. And so did I – for my idea of love. The trouble seems to be they weren't the same ideas. You see, Bill – I had more to give you – far more – than you ever wanted from me.

COLLYER. How can you say that? You know I wanted your love –

HESTER. No, Bill. You wanted me simply to be a loving wife. There's all the difference in the world.

Pause.

COLLYER. Do you imagine I believed that pathetic story just now about a studio and a job? Do you think I don't know exactly how you visualize your future? (HESTER *is silent.*) You'll never let him go, Hester. You can't. (HESTER *is still silent. Pleadingly.*) Hester, my darling, what you say about me and my feelings for you may be true, but I'm offering you your only chance of life. Why can't you accept? After all, it worked quite happily once.

HESTER. Yes, it did. Very happily.

COLLYER. Well, then?

HESTER *does not reply.* COLLYER *takes her and kisses her. She does not try to prevent him, but responds in no way at all. After a moment he releases her.*

HESTER. You see, Bill, I'm not any longer the same person.

Pause.

You'd better go.

COLLYER *looks away from her and his glance strays round the room.*

(*Impatiently.*) I'll be all right.

COLLYER *nods and goes to the door.*

COLLYER. You still want your divorce then?

HESTER. Yes, Bill. I think it would be best.

COLLYER. There'll be a lot to discuss – business things.

HESTER. Yes. I suppose there will.

COLLYER. For the moment are you all right for money?

HESTER. Please, Bill.

COLLYER. Goodbye, then.

HESTER. Goodbye.

He looks at her puzzled and deeply troubled. He seems to be considering making a final appeal. HESTER *turns from his gaze.* COLLYER *shrugs his shoulders and goes.* HESTER, *left alone, takes a sip of her wine. She is moving to sit down when the sound of a key in the lock makes her turn sharply. She moves back quickly into the recess formed by the kitchen, out of sight of the front door. This opens furtively to reveal* PHILIP WELCH. HESTER *comes out of the recess.*

HESTER. Freddie?

PHILIP *turns sharply. He seems acutely embarrassed.*

PHILIP. Oh.

HESTER. How did you get in?

PHILIP. It's Page . . . you see, he lent me a key . . . He wanted me to pick up his suitcase. He's got all his washing things in it, apparently, and says he needs them for tonight.

HESTER. Where's he going tonight?

PHILIP (*uncomfortably*). I don't know.

HESTER. Where is he now?

PHILIP. Er – I don't know what the place is called.

HESTER. Where is it?

PHILIP. Somewhere in the West End.

HESTER. Greek Street?

PHILIP (*stubbornly*). I don't know.

Pause.

HESTER. I see. How long have you been with him?

PHILIP. Since nine.

HESTER. And he can do a lot of talking in three hours –
especially when he's drunk.

PHILIP. He's not drunk. At least what he says makes sense.

HESTER (*bitterly*). Does it?

PHILIP (*in slightly avuncular tones*). Lady Collyer – may I
say something? Page has been very frank with me. Very
frank indeed, although I didn't invite his confidence. So I
know the whole situation you see, and I do understand what
you must be feeling at this moment –

HESTER. Do you, Mr. Welch?

PHILIP. I've been in love too, you know. In fact about a year
ago I nearly had a bust-up in *my* marriage – over a sort of
infatuation I had for a girl – quite the wrong sort of type,
really, and it would have been disastrous – but I do know
what it means to have to give someone up whom you –
think you love. Look – do you think this is awfully imper-
tinent of me?

HESTER. Not at all.

PHILIP (*emboldened*). Well, I do think you ought to – sort of –
try and steel yourself to what I'm quite sure is the best

course for both of you. Gosh, I know how hard it is, but I
do remember, with this girl – she was an actress you know,
although she wasn't well-known or anything – I just sat
down all alone one day and said to myself – look, on the
physical side, she's everything in the world you want.
On the other side – what is she? Nothing. So what I did was
to write her a letter – and then I went away for a fortnight
all by myself – and of course I had hell, but gradually
things got sort of clearer in my mind, and when I got back
I was out of the wood.

HESTER. I'm so glad. Where was it you went?

PHILIP. Lyme Regis.

HESTER. A very pretty spot. I know it.

PHILIP. Of course I think for you some place like Italy or the
South of France would be better.

HESTER. Why better than Lyme Regis?

PHILIP. Well, complete change of atmosphere, you know –
nice weather, nobody you know, and lots of time to think
things out. And I know if you do think things out honestly,
you'll see how awfully petty the whole thing really is –
when you get it in perspective. I mean, without trying to
be preachy or anything, it *is* really the spiritual values that
count in this life, isn't it? I mean the physical side is really
awfully unimportant – objectively speaking, don't you
think?

HESTER (*gravely*). Objectively speaking. (*She gets up
indicating dismissal.*) Well, it's very kind of you, Mr.
Welch, to give me this advice. I'm very grateful.

PHILIP. Oh, that's all right. I'm glad you didn't fly at me for
it. You see Page has been telling me about it all, and I was
really awfully interested, because a thing like this it's –
well – it throws a sort of light on human nature, really.

HESTER. Yes. I suppose it does.

PHILIP. Well, may I have the bag now, please?

HESTER. It's just through that door.

PHILIP goes into the bedroom, reappearing after a moment with a suitcase.

Where did Freddie tell you to take that bag? To a station or somewhere, or back to the White Angel?

PHILIP. Back to the White – (*He stops abruptly.*)

Pause.

(*Lamely.*) Back to where he is.

HESTER (*quietly*). Would you mind putting the bag down, please, and going?

PHILIP. I'm afraid I can't do that. I promised him I'd bring it to him, you see. Well, goodbye.

He turns towards the door. HESTER is there before him and quickly turns a key in the lock. She removes the key and puts it in her pocket, and she goes towards the telephone, where she turns up a telephone book.

HESTER. I'm sorry for that melodramatic gesture, but I've got to detain you for a moment or two, I'm afraid. (*She begins to dial a telephone number.*) I won't keep you long. There's the remains of a bottle of claret there, if you'd like it.

PHILIP (*stiffly*). No, thank you. (*He goes to the door.*)

HESTER. No, that key won't help you. It's a separate lock.

PHILIP (*angrily*). Look, I really do think –

HESTER. Please sit down. You've got a splendid chance now of resuming your study of human nature.

She is dialling a number. PHILIP stands watching her.

Hullo . . . White Angel? Is Mr. Page there? . . . (*Louder.*) Mr. Page . . . That's right . . . Oh, he is . . . Mrs. Jackson . . . no, Jackson . . . Yes. (*To PHILIP.*) There's a lot of noise in there. (*Pause.*) Hullo? . . . Darling, it's Hester – don't ring off. No scene, I promise . . . I promise, I promise. I only want to know about the job, that's all . . . (*Louder.*) The job . . . Did you see the man? . . . Oh good . . . Oh good . . .

I see. Well done. How soon? . . . As soon as that? . . . Oh,
Freddie . . . no, I'm sorry. It was just hearing you say it like
that – that's all . . . (*Louder.*) It was just hearing you say
it . . . Look, your messenger is here for your bag – only it
hasn't got half of what you want for three days. Where are
you going to until you leave? . . . No, that's all right. Don't
tell me, if you don't want to. I only meant country or town?
Now, let's think. You've got your flannels in the bag so
you'll just want your tweed coat . . . All right. What did you
want done with the rest of your things? . . . Oh, when did
you post it? . . . I'll get it tomorrow then . . . The cloakroom
at Charing Cross . . . I see . . . Yes. I'll do that . . . Look,
Freddie, I want you to do one last thing for me . . . I said
I wanted you to do one last thing. Come and collect your
bag yourself . . . just to say goodbye, that's all. Surely
there's no harm . . . No. I won't, I won't. I promise I won't.
I swear to you, on my most sacred word of honour, I won't
try and make you stay. I won't even talk, if you don't want
me to. You can just take your bag and go . . . I want to see
you again, that's all . . . Freddie, trust me, trust me, for
pity's sake . . . Freddie, don't ring off – don't –

*She looks blankly at the receiver, and then replaces it. She
stares at it a moment, evidently wondering whether to dial
again, and then decides it would be useless. She goes slowly
to the door, puts the key in the lock, and unlocks it, indicating to* PHILIP *with a gesture that he is free to go.*

PHILIP (*hesitating*). Didn't you say something about a tweed
coat?

HESTER. Did I? Oh yes. It's hanging up on that door.

PHILIP *goes into the bedroom, carrying the suitcase.*
HESTER, *left alone, wanders towards the mantelpiece. She
looks down at the gas-fire.* PHILIP *reappears with a tweed
coat over his arm.*

PHILIP (*on his way to the door*). Well – good night.

HESTER. Good night, Mr. Welch. Oh, by the way, your wife is
rather worried about you. Perhaps you'd better slip up and
see her before you go out again.

PHILIP. Yes. I will. (*Earnestly.*) You're all right alone, aren't you? I mean, you're not going to do anything silly tonight. You must have learnt your lesson from last night.

HESTER. Yes. I've learnt my lesson.

PHILIP. I'm awfully sorry – really I am.

HESTER. Thank you.

PHILIP. I think he ought to have come to fetch his things himself.

HESTER. So do I.

PHILIP. Although of course I understood him not wanting to come round when he thought you might try and stop him, but – still – after you gave him your sacred, solemn word of honour just now –

HESTER *has not previously been looking at* PHILIP. *She now turns slowly to face him.*

HESTER. It might add a little to your appreciation of spiritual values, Mr. Welch, if I told you that I hadn't the smallest intention of keeping that sacred, solemn word of honour. If Freddie had come here tonight, I would have made him stay. Of course he knew that perfectly well, and that's why he wouldn't come.

PHILIP, *shocked, stares at her in silence.* HESTER *looks up at him.*

HESTER. You've got exactly the same expression on your face that my father would have had if I'd said that to him. He believed in spiritual values, too, you know – and the pettiness of the physical side.

Pause.

Take the bag to Freddie now. Have you got enough money for a taxi?

PHILIP. Yes, thank you. (*At the door.*) Can I – should I give Page any sort of message from you or anything?

Pause.

HESTER (*quietly*). Just my love.

PHILIP *nods and goes.* HESTER *closes the door after him. After a second of utter stillness she moves quietly to the window, and gently closes it. Then she goes to her bag and searches for a coin. Not finding what she is looking for she turns quickly to the table on to which* FREDDIE *had thrown the shilling. She picks it up and walks to the gas meter, inserts the coin, and we hear it drop. She turns to the front-door and locks it. Then she places a rug carefully on the floor against the door. Turning, she picks up the empty bottle of aspirin, looks at it, and puts it down. Then she pulls from her pocket the sleeping pills given her by* MILLER, *takes a glass from the table, goes into the kitchen, and reappears having filled it with water. Her breath is now coming in short gasps, as if she had been undergoing some strong physical exertion, although her movements until now have not been hurried. There is a knock on the door, arresting her in the action of putting the pills into her mouth.*

(*Impatiently.*) Yes? Who is it?

MILLER (*off*). Miller.

HESTER. What do you want? I'm just going to bed.

MILLER (*off*). I want to see you.

HESTER. Won't it keep to the morning?

MILLER (*off*). No.

HESTER *impatiently goes to the door, pulls the rug up, and throws it on to the sofa where it falls to the floor. She unlocks the door and lets* MILLER *in.*

(*Indicating key.*) Determined not to be disturbed?

HESTER. I usually lock my door at night.

MILLER. It's lucky you didn't last night.

HESTER (*indicating the glass of water*). I was just going to take your pills.

MILLER. So I see.

HESTER. Do you think they're strong enough, Doctor. Could you let me have another two or three in case they don't work?

MILLER, *without replying, picks up the rug from the floor and puts it on the sofa. Then, watched by* HESTER, *he strolls to the gas-fire and with a casual flick of his foot, kicks on the tap. We hear the hiss of escaping gas. He kicks it off.*

I said could you let me have –

MILLER. I heard you. The answer is no.

HESTER. Why not?

MILLER. I've been involved enough with the police. I don't want to be accused now of giving drugs to a suicidal patient. (*He holds out his hand.*)

HESTER. Aren't you letting your imagination run away with you, Doctor?

MILLER. No. I want those pills back, please.

HESTER. Why?

MILLER. If you put a rug down in front of a door it's wiser to do it when the lights are out.

HESTER (*hysterically*). Why are you spying on me? Why can't you leave me alone?

MILLER. I'm not trying to decide for you whether you live or die. That choice is yours and you have quite enough courage to make it for yourself –

HESTER (*with a despairing cry*). Courage!

MILLER. Oh yes. It takes courage to condemn yourself to death. Most suicides die to escape. *You're* dying because you feel unworthy to live. Isn't that true?

HESTER (*wildly*). How do I know what's true? I only know that after tonight I won't be able to face life any more.

MILLER. What is there so hard about facing life? Most people seem to be able to manage it.

HESTER. How can anyone live without hope?

MILLER. Quite easily. To live without hope can mean to live without despair.

HESTER. Those are just words.

MILLER. Words can help you if your mind can only grasp them. (*He twists her roughly round to face him. Harshly.*) Your Freddie has left you. He's never going to come back again. Never in the world. Never.

At each word she wilts as if at a physical blow.

HESTER (*wildly*). I know. I know. That's what I can't face.

MILLER (*with brutal force*). Yes, you can. That word 'never'. Face that and you can face life. Get beyond hope. It's your only chance.

HESTER. What is there beyond hope?

MILLER. Life. You must believe that. It's true – I know.

HESTER*'s storm of tears is subsiding. She raises her head to look at him.*

HESTER (*at length*). You can still find some purpose in living.

MILLER. What purpose?

HESTER. You have your work at the hospital.

MILLER. For me the only purpose in life is to live it. My work at the hospital is a help to me in that. That is all. If you looked perhaps you might also find some help for yourself.

HESTER. What help?

MILLER. Haven't you got your work too? (*He makes a gesture towards the paintings.*)

HESTER. Oh that. (*Wearily.*) There's no escape for me through that.

MILLER. Not through that, or that. (*With a wide gesture he indicates the later paintings.*) But perhaps through that. (*He points to the early painting.*) I'm not an art expert, but

I believe there was talent here. Just a spark, that's all, which with a little feeding, might have become a little flame. Not a great fire, which could have illumined the world – oh no – I'm not saying that. But the world is a dark enough place for even a little flicker to be welcome.

He hands her a glass of water, which she drinks. Then he turns back to the picture.

I'd like to buy that.

HESTER *gazes at the picture listlessly for a moment. Then she gets up wearily, goes to the picture, and hands it to him. He smiles.*

How much?

HESTER. It's a gift.

MILLER *shakes his head, still smiling. He pulls out his wallet and removes two pound notes.* HESTER *shakes her head.* MILLER *puts the notes on the table.*

MILLER. Look. I'm going to put these notes down here. It's what I can afford to give you – not what I think the picture's worth. If you're determined not to sell it, slip the notes into an envelope and address them to me. I shall understand, and be sorry. Good night.

HESTER. Good night, Doctor.

MILLER *(turning)*. Not Doctor, please.

Pause.

HESTER. Good night, my friend.

MILLER. I could wish that you meant that.

HESTER *(quietly)*. What makes you so sure that I don't mean it?

MILLER *(also quietly)*. I hope that I may be given a proof that you do – by tomorrow morning.

HESTER. Are you asking me to make my choice in order to help you?

MILLER (*smiling*). Surely I have a right to feel sad if I lose a new-found friend – especially one whom I so much like and respect.

HESTER (*bitterly*). Respect?

MILLER. Yes, respect.

HESTER. Please, don't be too kind to me.

He approaches her quickly and takes her shoulders.

MILLER. Listen to me. To see yourself as the world sees you may be very brave, but it can also be very foolish. Why should you accept the world's view of you as a weak-willed neurotic – better dead than alive? What right have they to judge? To judge you they must have the capacity to feel as you feel. And who has? One in a thousand. You alone know how you have felt. And you alone know how unequal the battle has always been that your will has had to fight.

HESTER. 'I tried to be good and failed.' Isn't that the excuse that all criminals make?

MILLER. When they make it justly, it's a just excuse.

HESTER. Does it let them escape the sentence?

MILLER. Yes, if the judge is fair – and not blind with hatred for the criminal – as you are for yourself.

HESTER. If you could find me one extenuating circumstance – one single reason why I should respect myself – even a little.

The door is abruptly thrown open and FREDDIE *appears on the threshold.*

FREDDIE. Hullo.

HESTER. Hullo.

Pause.

MILLER (*to* HESTER). You must find that reason for yourself.

He touches her hand, nods to FREDDIE, *and goes.*

FREDDIE. Did I interrupt something?

HESTER. No. Not really.

FREDDIE. He seems quite a good bloke, old Miller.

HESTER. Yes. He does. Did you come for your bag?

FREDDIE. Yes.

HESTER. That boy took it with him.

FREDDIE. Oh. Well, he'll leave it at the Angel. I'll get it all right.

HESTER. Come in, Freddie. Don't stand in the door.

FREDDIE *shuffles in.*

How are you feeling now?

FREDDIE. All right.

HESTER. Thank you for coming.

FREDDIE. I shouldn't have sent the kid anyway, I suppose.

HESTER. Had any food?

FREDDIE. Yes. I had a bite at the Belvedere. What about you?

HESTER. Oh, I'll get myself something later.

There is a pause, while FREDDIE *still watches her apprehensively.*

When exactly are you off to Rio?

FREDDIE. Thursday. I told you.

HESTER. Oh yes, of course. By boat?

FREDDIE. Oh no. Flying.

HESTER. Oh yes, of course. By the Azores, isn't it?

FREDDIE. No. London, West Africa – then across to Natal.

HESTER. Sounds exciting.

FREDDIE. Oh, I don't know. Oh, by the way – about the rent. My golf clubs will fetch thirty or forty quid. They'll take care of old Ma Elton and a few odd bills.

HESTER. Won't you need them?

FREDDIE. No. I can't fly them.

HESTER. I'll pack the rest of your things tonight and get them round to Charing Cross in the morning.

FREDDIE. No hurry.

Pause.

What are you going to do, Hes?

HESTER. I'm not quite sure yet, Freddie. I think I'll stay on here for a bit.

FREDDIE. I dropped a note in at Bill's house. He'll probably be round.

HESTER. He's been round.

FREDDIE. Oh. Are you – ?

HESTER. No.

FREDDIE. I'm sorry.

HESTER. It's all right. It wouldn't have worked.

FREDDIE. No. I suppose not. I didn't know. You'll go on with your painting, will you?

HESTER. Yes. I think so. As a matter of fact I might even go to an Art School, and start from the beginning again.

FREDDIE. Good idea. It's never too late to begin again. Isn't that what they say?

HESTER. Yes. They do.

There is a long pause. FREDDIE *seems to be waiting for* HESTER *to say something, but she stands quite still, looking at him.*

FREDDIE (*at length*). Well –

HESTER (*in a clear, calm voice*). Goodbye, Freddie.

Pause.

FREDDIE (*murmuring*). Goodbye, Hes.

He moves to the door. HESTER *still does not move.*
FREDDIE *turns, waiting for her to say something. She
does not. He suddenly walks up to her.*

Thank you for everything.

HESTER. Thank you, too.

*He kisses her. She accepts the embrace without in any way
returning it.*

FREDDIE. I'm going to miss you, Hes.

After a moment, FREDDIE *releases her, goes to the door,
and turns round, still with a faint air of bewildered appeal.*

HESTER (*loudly and clearly*). Goodbye.

FREDDIE *stares at her, turns, and shuffles out, closing the
door.* HESTER *stands rigid, her face utterly expressionless.
Then she moves quickly across the room and reaches up
for a suitcase which is on a shelf above the bedroom
door. She puts the suitcase – which is labelled* F. T. PAGE –
on a chair, and goes across to collect those clothes of
FREDDIE'S *that are hanging on the pegs by the front-door.
As she begins to take these down, methodically, one by one,
she appears momentarily to lose her hard composure.
She buries her face in his mackintosh, and remains so for
a few brief seconds. Then she roughly pulls the mackintosh
down from the hook and throws it and the other clothes on
to the sofa.*

*The light seems to hurt her eyes. She turns out all but a
reading lamp. Then she goes to the fire, turns on the gas,
and lights it with a match. She stands by the fire for a
moment, watching the flame change from orange to red. She
has turned back to the sofa, and is quietly folding one of*
FREDDIE'S *scarves as the curtain falls.*

The End.